REVIEW, REIMAGINE, RENEW:

Mission making a difference in a changing world

Edited by Gabrielle McMullen, Patrice Scales and Denis Fitzgerald

Published in 2016 by Connor Court Publishing Pty Ltd

Copyright © Catholic Social Services, Victoria

All rights reserved. No part of this book may be reproduced or transmitted in any form or by any means, electronic or mechanical, including photocopying, recording or by any information storage and retrieval system, without prior permission in writing from the publisher.

Connor Court Publishing Pty Ltd
PO Box 7257
Redland Bay QLD 4165
Australia

sales@connorcourt.com
www.connorcourt.com

Phone 0497-900-685

ISBN: 978-1-925501-22-3

Cover design: Rita Terunawidjaja

Printed in Australia

TABLE OF CONTENTS

Preface *Bishop Mark Edwards OMI*   5

Introduction *Gabrielle McMullen, Patrice Scales and Denis Fitzgerald*   7

Review, Re-imagine and Renew: Reflections on Mission

Pope Francis: A Magna Carta for Catholic Social Services   21
John L Allen Jnr

Mission Making a Difference in a Changing World   35
Maria Harries with Jayne Lloyd, Al Curtain, Deb Tsorbaris and John Falzon

Pope Francis, Catholic Social Teaching and the Right to Migrate   47
Frank Brennan SJ

2016 Mary MacKillop Oration *Julian McMahon*   61

Heart and Head Together for Action *Julie Edwards*   71

Mission in the Changing World: Challenges to the Church

Confronting Family Violence: A Challenge for the Church to Make a Difference   *Helen Burt and Patrice Scales with Bishop Vincent Long OFMConv*   83

Addressing and Preventing Sexual Abuse   97
Gabrielle McMullen with Robert Fitzgerald and Maria Harries

The Mission or the Money or Both *Tony Nicholson*   115

Mission-Inspired Responses to a Changing Environment *Ricki Jeffrey*   125

Mission Making a Difference: Responses to Vulnerable People

Making a Real Difference to Poverty *Marcelle Mogg*   135

Putting Child Safety First *Gerard Jones and Ché Stockley*   147

Challenges in Advocacy and Support for Recently Arrived Refugees   159
Tomasa Morales

Learning from the NDIS Pilot: The Experience of CatholicCare   165
Canberra & Goulburn *Anne Kirwan with Helen Burt*

Care of Older People from the Margins: The Trauma-Informed   175
Approach at Sacred Heart Mission *Stephen Schmidtke and Marija Dragic
with Michael Yore*

More than Giving Back: Maximising the Mission Impact of Volunteers   189
Lisa McDonald

Conclusion *Denis Fitzgerald*   197

Contributors   205
Acknowledgements   221

Preface

Bishop Mark Edwards OMI

Social services are about the disadvantaged and the hurting, and can never be primarily about building an empire or making a comfortable life for ourselves or our employees.

In Catholic social services only Jesus can be the cornerstone. He calls us to be with him and to care for others. He teaches us about encounter, compassion and care, and supports us in that.

Encounter, compassion and care are more than indispensable. They are at the heart of all our work. Tolerance is the secular version of love, I think. But it is not sufficient as a Catholic value, ever. The rich man tolerated Lazarus. He did not persecute him, drive him from his door or set the dogs on him. However, neither did he encounter him. Compassion was conspicuously absent. The rich man did not open his eyes to see Lazarus. Our call is to know the people with whom we work and out of that connection comes real care and our best work.

While it takes effort, time and money to lead our staff to identify their mission with Christ and his Church, this is an important task. I believe that if we get our identity right, many difficulties in our mission will be solved. If we do not get our identity right, we will not be able to get our mission right either.

It is a tough time to be a Catholic at the moment. It is harder than it should be for many in social services to do good because of the evil actions of some priests and the inaction of some bishops. I apologise to you and to those who work with you for that. The only good reason to be a Catholic is because we believe it to be the best way to be close to Jesus. I thank those in Catholic social services for their commitment.

*****

The *Review, Reimagine, Renew* conference in February 2016 was a rewarding time. One risk of such experiences is that what we hear on one occasion only does not have an opportunity to penetrate and so might leave us largely unchanged. This book will keep the conference's insights before our eyes for long enough for us to integrate them into our lives.

As John Allen pointed out, Pope Francis is pushing the Church towards those at the peripheries; he is a missionary and his motto literally is mercy. As people involved in the Church's social ministries the wind is at our back, though, as mentioned, this is a tough time to be Catholic in Australia in other ways. The Church is calling for missionaries of mercy; let us seize the moment. In this Jubilee Year of Mercy, we are being challenged to give people what they need, not what they deserve, and to do this to the extent of being like the Father.

Mary Jo Leddy in *Radical Gratitude*[1] tells the story of how a refugee, by mistaking Mary Jo's garage for a house, led her to see her world in a new way. She had a house for her car! From this moment, the days of her car being off the road and under cover were numbered. I wonder what 'houses for cars' there might be in our lives. May the gift of seeing our world through God's eyes be given to us.

Being at *Review, Reimagine, Renew* was an effective way for us to support each other. I thank those who were able to attend for making that effort and supporting each other, and all involved in Catholic social services for their care and love for the vulnerable. I am variously deeply moved, encouraged, given hope and challenged by your work.

May the gift from God of seeing aspects of our mission anew, offered and received at *Review, Reimagine, Renew*, become a part of our lives.

---

[1] M.J. Leddy, 2002. *Radical Gratitude*. New York: Orbis Books, pp.14-16.

Introduction

Gabrielle McMullen, Patrice Scales and Denis Fitzgerald

In an environment of rapid and significant change and numerous challenges for Catholic social services and other ministries, leaders, practitioners and supporters need to be equipped to set new directions wisely, make difficult decisions, and build their networks for mission-impact. Critically important in this endeavour is exploring and deepening our understanding of 'mission' in this challenging new world.

On 24-26 February 2016 over 250 participants from across Australia gathered at the Catholic Leadership Centre in Melbourne for the 2016 Catholic Social Services conference entitled *Review, Reimagine, Renew: Mission making a difference in a changing world*. Exploring and responding to the implications of 'mission' underpinned the 2016 conference, which built on the successful 2013 conference, *Listening, Learning and Leading: The impact of Catholic identity and mission on what we do and how we do it*.[2]

Review, Reimagine, Renew

Like its predecessor, the 2016 conference engaged with contemporary themes to empower participants to approach renewal in Catholic social services underpinned by both the timeless message of the Gospels and the necessary innovation for effective ministry in a changing environment. Issues addressed by the conference included, in the Australian context, institutional child abuse, family violence, engagement with Indigenous Australians, offering disability services, supporting re-settlement, and breaking the poverty cycle and, in the wider international setting, the situation of refugees and asylum seekers and capital

---

[2] Papers from the 2013 conference are available in G. McMullen and J. Warhurst (eds), 2014. *Listening, Learning and Leading: The Impact of Catholic Identity and Mission*. Ballarat: Connor Court.

punishment. Across all these themes, and expressed in a variety of ways, the focus was on how our response should be shaped by our call to bring the "compassionate gaze of Christ"[3] to disadvantaged and vulnerable people.

These themes, addressed through conference lectures, panels and workshops, were welcomed by participants as relevant to their needs and conference presentations, capturing the essence of Catholic ministries responding to the "signs of the times",[4] were insightful and challenging for participants. Catholic Social Services Victoria therefore thought that it would be valuable to make the content of the conference available to a wider audience. To that end, conference presentations were re-written as stand-alone chapters for publication in this volume.

Like the conference, this volume challenges us individually and as agencies. As individuals, we are challenged to deepen our understanding of what it is to be a leader in Christian social services in Australia today; we are challenged:

- to review our personal calling to the ministry of Jesus, to put ourselves "permanently in a state of mission" (as Pope Francis puts it),[5]

- to re-imagine the Gospel imperatives in the contemporary context, and to renew our organisations so that we bring all the dimensions of the "joy of the Gospel" to those whom we serve.[6]

Mission making a difference

The particular mission of Catholic Social Services Victoria is "to assist the Catholic Church in Victoria to fulfil the gospel imperatives:

---

[3] Pope Benedict XVI, 2006. Message for Lent 2006. Vatican City: Vatican; accessed on 4 May 2016 at w2.vatican.va.

[4] Pope Paul VI, 1965. *Gaudium et Spes: Pastoral Constitution on the Church in the Modern World*, Section 4. Vatican City: Vatican; accessed on 3 May 2016 at www.vatican.va.

[5] Pope Francis, 2013. Apostolic Exhortation: *Evangelii Gaudium*, Section 25. Vatican City: Vatican; accessed on 3 May 2016 at w2.vatican.va.

[6] Ibid., Section 1.

to stand with and serve the poor, disadvantaged and marginalised, and to work for a just, equitable and compassionate society".[7]

The mission of Catholic Social Services Australia is that it "advances the social service ministry which is integral to the Mission of the Catholic Church in Australia".[8]

In both cases, this mission is the advancement of the Gospel call to love of neighbour, in the context of our contemporary society.

This mission is, in fact, shared by the whole Catholic social services sector, by individual Catholic social service agencies as well as by the peak bodies within the sector. One of the main contributions by the peak bodies to the advancement of this mission is raising the awareness of leaders across the sector of the various dimensions of this mission, to their personal engagement with mission, and to their understanding of the implications of this mission for everyone within their organisations.

'Formation' is a term for such personal development, and for generations this term has resonated with people who have been 'formed' within religious congregations or similar. However, one of the challenges within the sector today is that many of those who have governance, leadership, practitioner and other key roles do not have a background associated with such formation. Indeed, quite a number of those who contribute to the mission of Catholic social services are not themselves Catholic. The term 'formation' itself is not, one can assume, widely understood without explanation.

But under whatever heading, for the peak Catholic Social Services bodies, a key means of realising their challenging mission is offering formation for mission to leaders in their member agencies as well as to the wider Catholic social services sector. The 2016 conference was one such activity and attracted participants from around Australia and from a range of other Church ministries as well as social services.

---

[7] For information on Catholic Social Services Victoria, see www.css.org.au; accessed on 3 May 2016.
[8] For information on Catholic Social Services Australia, see www.cssa.org.au; accessed on 4 July 2016

The importance of formation for mission

Pope Francis, in the first homily following his election, reminded us that "we can build many things, but if we do not profess Jesus Christ, things go wrong. We may become a charitable NGO, but not the Church".[9]

This is a particular challenge to Catholic social service ministries as they work to further the social mission of the Gospels. Their *raison d'être* is the Gospel call to feed the hungry, welcome the stranger, clothe the naked, care for the sick, visit those in prison (*Matthew* 25:35-36). Our Catholic agencies continue the ministry of Jesus in contemporary society, especially seeking to emulate his service of the poor and vulnerable.

And yet so much of what we do, such as service to those who are aged or with a disability, housing and support for people who are homeless, drug and alcohol treatment, transition programs for those in prison and so on, is also done by organisations that are not Catholic or Christian.

There are many dimensions to Catholic identity, but Pope Francis is clearly challenging us to ensure that a distinctive feature of our work is that we go beyond what other agencies would offer, that we bring the loving presence of Jesus to those whom we serve. Our Catholic identity is not only in what we do, but in how we do it; we must minister with love, in humility, as we would serve our God, just as our God cares for us.[10]

All of those who serve in our ministries, whether Catholics or not, need to be formed for ministry as well as having current qualifications and/or experience for their professional or governance role.

If this is our aspiration, if this is indeed needed for our agencies to be faithful to their Catholic identity and mission, those who work there need professional development beyond their specific professional learning. For this 'calling', they need ongoing formation for mission.

The critical importance of formation for those in Catholic social

---

[9] Pope Francis, 2013. Homily, *Missa Pro Ecclesia* with the Cardinal Electors. Vatican City: Vatican; accessed on 3 May 2016 at www.vatican.va.

[10] For a contemporary exploration of this issue, see M. Yore, 2016. 'Having An Impact: Do Social Services Shaped by Catholic Identity Make a Difference? A Catholic Social Services Victoria Occasional Paper' at www.css.org.au; accessed on 5 July 2016.

services was highlighted by Pope Benedict XVI in *Deus Caritas Est*. Designating them 'charity workers', he stated:

> … while professional competence is a primary, fundamental requirement, it is not of itself sufficient. We are dealing with human beings, and human beings always need something more than technically proper care. They need humanity. They need heartfelt concern. Those who work for the Church's charitable organizations must be distinguished by the fact that they do not merely meet the needs of the moment, but they dedicate themselves to others with heartfelt concern, enabling them to experience the richness of their humanity. Consequently, in addition to their necessary professional training, these charity workers need a 'formation of the heart': they need to be led to that encounter with God in Christ which awakens their love and opens their spirits to others. As a result, love of neighbour will no longer be for them a commandment imposed, so to speak, from without, but a consequence deriving from their faith, a faith which becomes active through love.[11]

More recently, Pope Francis has reminded us that formation for those who work in Catholic ministries must be well-defined and ongoing. "We cannot improvise. We must take this seriously",[12] he says and, for mission, we are "called constantly to improve and to grow in communion, holiness and wisdom".[13]

The challenge for Catholic social services in Australia, with their pluralist workforces at all levels, is to provide this "formation of the heart", and to enable our people to grow in "communion, holiness and wisdom", even though many do not identify as Catholic.

The *Review, Reimagine, Renew* conference was such a formation engagement, as was its 2013 predecessor.

They engaged with the sector as it is: large and small organisations, in city and regional locations, offering services across the spectrum of

---

[11] Pope Benedict XVI, 2005. Encyclical Letter, *Deus Caritas Est*, Section 31. Vatican City: Vatican; accessed on 3 May 2016 at w2.vatican.va.

[12] Pope Francis, 2014. Address to participants in the plenary session of the Congregation for Catholic Education. Vatican City: Vatican; accessed on 3 May 2016 at w2.vatican.va.

[13] Pope Francis, 2015. Presentation of Christmas greetings to the Roman Curia. Vatican City: Vatican; accessed on 3 May 2016 at w2.vatican.va.

human need and with people who, while contributing to the mission of Catholic social services, are doing so from various points on the spectrum of personal faith commitment.

Thus, the Catholic Social Services conference, in addressing key challenges and agendas for the sector, and also by means of its liturgies and occasions for formal and informal interaction and exchange, offered participants formation as it explored ways of continuing to make a positive difference to our society and to those most in need.

The following sections of this Introduction, corresponding to the three parts of the book, summarise the key topics of the conference as addressed by the authors of the subsequent chapters who were, for the most part, speakers in conference plenary lecture, panel and workshop sessions.

Part 1: Review, Re-imagine and Renew: Reflections on Mission

The first section of this book brings together a number of reflections on mission, almost all very personal and certainly from the point of view of the lived experience of each of the contributors.

John Allen looks beyond the 'celebrity' of Pope Francis and reminds us that an understanding of Pope Francis' leadership on mission is firmly embedded in three pillars: a passion for those on the peripheries, a deeply missionary concept of Church and, thirdly, mercy as the cornerstone spiritual message the world needs to hear from the Church at this moment in time. Allen says that if we understand these three pillars we will understand 90 percent of everything the Pope says and does. The takeaway, says Allen, is that in Pope Francis we have, in effect, a Magna Carta for Catholic social services in flesh and bone. It is an entertaining and insightful contribution into what could be seen as the Pope's vision for the Church: a heartfelt plea for the Church to get out of the sacristy and into the streets.

The forum on mission making a difference in a changing world brought together practitioners who reflected on the challenge of living out mission in the services they and their organisations provide. In this paper, they remind us that integrating mission into core work is not easy in the world in which we are working, with its increasing complexity and inequality, while balancing the demanding expectations of 'organisational professionalism', diminishing government funding and increasing regulation. The Cardijn principles of 'see, judge, act' and the lived principles of Catholic Social Teaching are highlighted in the forum's discussion, as is the need to live out the practice of faith and the Eucharist. The need for critical thinking, for activism, for never remaining silent, and for always being people of hope imbues these interesting reflections.

Professor Frank Brennan SJ melds the themes of Catholic Social Teaching and the right to migrate in his paper. As Brennan reflects, recent popes, including John Paul II, Benedict XVI and Francis, have wrestled with what constitutes a just reason for emigrating to a country not one's own. Brennan particularly draws on the example set by Pope Francis in opening his arms and heart to the plight of the poor, the sick, those with disabilities and asylum seekers. Brennan sees Francis' words and actions around asylum seekers and migrants as the Pope's challenge to both individual citizens and legislators to extend mercy across all barriers. Whether it was the Pope's visit to Lampedusa, the US-Mexico border or the Greek island of Lesbos, Brennan writes that Francis provides those of goodwill with the incentive and inspiration to revisit Catholic Social Teaching on migration.

In his Mary MacKillop Oration dinner address, Julian McMahon reflected briefly on the importance of respect and courtesy in all our relationships, noting that we all lose something when we do not have a common understanding of what the words mean. It was, however, the word 'courage' about which he chose to speak: the courage of two Australians, Myuran Sukumaran and Andrew Chan, as they stood against the 'machinery of death', and refused to sign their own death warrants unless their content was true. It was a hushed room of 200 people who listened to McMahon recount the events of that day, saying that the term 'speaking truth to power' was never more apt than at this time. A reading of McMahon's presentation will similarly keep you spellbound, and reflecting on the sacredness of life.

In 'Heart and Head Together for Action', the final keynote address of the conference, Julie Edwards reminds us that as Catholic social service organisations, we do not necessarily have a monopoly on goodness or virtue. At a time when the Church is under scrutiny for its shocking history of sexual abuse by priests and religious, and its cover-ups, we must question whether we are producing the fruit of the kingdom of God. In the Ignatian tradition, she notes that, in bringing heart and head together for action, we must enter a process of discernment and reflection. That reflection is always for the purpose of action. God is active in the world, creating, loving and sustaining it, and we are called to be part of this action.

Part 2: Mission in the Changing World: Challenges to the Church

The contributions in this section of the book canvas some of the broad and critical challenges, both to the Church and social service organisations, on a number of mission fronts. Each topic reminds us of the difficult path that the Church and Catholic social service organisations face now and in the future, but the spirit of Christ in addressing the challenges is inspiring, as the papers show.

The public forum on 'Confronting Family Violence: A Challenge for the Church to Make a Difference' was held to launch the following two-day *Review, Reimagine, Renew* conference. It brought together five experienced practitioners and advocates in the area of family violence who each contributed insightful, thought-provoking and frank opinions to the forum. Bishop Vincent Long OFMConv then offered a response on behalf of the Catholic Church at the conclusion of the forum. While the Church has responded to domestic violence in some very supportive ways in the past, Bishop Long reminds us that sadly there have been countless times when we have let women and children down. This paper very clearly sets out the challenge for the Church to make a difference.

Robert Fitzgerald and Maria Harries bring quite remarkable 'insider' contributions to the chapter on 'Addressing and Preventing Sexual Abuse'. It is clear from this paper that future work for the Catholic Church and its ministries must encompass a three-fold approach. There must be full recognition and acknowledgement of past evils and the way they were addressed, survivors must be treated with compassion and fairness and in great humility, and we must create for those in our care a safe environment that will prevent further abuse.

The challenge of balancing mission and money is the focus of Tony Nicholson's paper which explores the risk that mission-driven organisations take when they become too removed from the local communities they serve. He urges us to consider whether the current paradigm of contracting to government, larger organisations, efficiency gains, regulation and professionalisation will necessarily enable us to meet ever-increasing and emerging needs.

Ricki Jeffrey outlines the journey that Centacare Central Queensland took to move its workforce from not only being 'passion-driven' but also 'mission-driven'. As Jeffrey notes, its story demonstrates a greater understanding of how mission looks in every day actions in a social service-based organisation that is primarily government-funded with services delivered by a workforce of diverse traditions.

Part 3: Mission Making a Difference: Responses to Vulnerable People

Despite the challenges and the ever-changing environment, the Church's mission to care for the vulnerable, the poor and the disadvantaged has not diminished. As the contributions in this section show, when mission is aligned with service provision, the benefits to those we serve in Christ's name have far-greater impact.

Marcelle Mogg draws on the 'Dropping Off The Edge 2015' research into poverty in Australia to illustrate the complex interplay of factors that trap people and whole communities in situations of disadvantage. One can see links here with Tony Nicholson's view that local context is crucial when it comes to the provision of services. The solution to poverty can emerge from within the community if that community is allowed to contribute.

In its important paper, MacKillop Family Services shares its approach to child-safe standards in the 'Putting Child Safety First' contribution.

Central to MacKillop's development of a child-safe environment and framework has been the implementation of the Sanctuary Model, which acknowledges that to thrive and grow we need to feel safe. This is not an easy 'tick-the-box' compliance approach, but is one where the whole organisation must be engaged and responsible for keeping children safe.

For recently arrived refugees, often from traumatic backgrounds, the smallest acts of assistance and support can make a difference in navigating a completely new country, culture, language and systems. Tomasa Morales uses examples that remind us of the enormous difficulties facing newly-arrived migrants. But, as the paper on 'Challenges in Advocacy and Support for Recently Arrived Refugees' reminds us, advocacy at the public, government and policy levels is critically important. Advocacy, however, must also be done sensitively and in the interests of the refugees.

The National Disability Insurance Scheme (NDIS) has been heralded as a great step forward in Australia in providing client-directed support for people with disabilities. But for disability support organisations, implementation of the NDIS can be somewhat fraught with confusion, anxiety and fear. Anne Kirwan's paper provides some of the missing clarity and shows that the NDIS can be implemented while still retaining a focus on mission.

The link between trauma and homelessness and the provision of aged care is the subject of the paper 'Care of Older People from the Margins'. Sacred Heart Mission, which has long provided support for people experiencing homelessness, had its origins in a parish-based meals program. Through a Trauma and Homelessness Initiative, the Mission has focused on how its services can be better adapted to the provision of aged care support and accommodation, tailored specifically to the needs of people who have experienced entrenched social exclusion because of homelessness.

There could be no better way to end this section of this book on mission than to recognise and understand the importance of volunteers in promoting the mission of the organisations for which they work. As Lisa McDonald writes in 'More than Giving Back: Maximising the Mission Impact of Volunteers', the impact of volunteers on the mission of an organisation is not singular; it is rich, diverse and multi-layered.

Conclusion

Both the 2016 Catholic Social Services conference and the preparation of this volume occurred during the Jubilee Year of Mercy declared by Pope Francis. Significantly in his 2013 book titled *The Name of God is Mercy*, he stated that 'mercy is God's identity card'.[14] In the Year of Mercy this message offers a timely reminder to those in Catholic social services that mercy is also an integral part of their Catholic identity and living out the social mission of the Gospels.

---

[14] Pope Francis, 2013. *The Name of God is Mercy*. New York: Random House, p. 9.

Review, Re-imagine and Renew:

Reflections on Mission

Pope Francis: A Magna Carta for Catholic Social Services

John L Allen Jr

If you have a right to expect anything from a journalist, and frankly I would counsel you not to expect very much, it is that a journalist should always get her or his facts right.

And so I begin with a fact, not a hunch, not a theory, not an anecdotal impression, not a gut-level instinct but a hard-core, take it to the bank, hang your hat on it, empirical fact: as I write this in April 2016, Pope Francis is by far the most popular spiritual figure on the planet and one of the most popular figures of any time.

The popularity of Pope Francis

I could demonstrate the facticity of that claim to you in a variety of different ways. For example, we could start with the Pope's Twitter following. In terms of the combined volume of his nine Twitter accounts, Pope Francis is coming up on the 30,000,000 mark. This now makes him by far the most followed spiritual figure in the Twitter universe, easily surpassing the Dali Lama, for example.

He is not yet the most followed human being absolutely; that is Katy Perry. Rounding out the top five, all but one being entertainers, are: Justin Bieber, Barack Obama, Taylor Swift and Lady Gaga – surely the Apocalypse cannot be far behind! But give the Pope a break; he has only been on Twitter three years. Those folks have been around longer.

For another demonstration of the Pope's mass appeal, we can talk about his poll numbers. Again, it is a fact, not a theory, that in every corner of the world where public opinion can be scientifically measured this Pope has poll numbers that politicians and celebrities envy.

Think about this: after Pope Francis' trip to the United States last

September there was a Gallup *USA Today* poll which found that overall the Pope had an 80 percent approval rating in America among Americans generally and a 92 percent approval rating among American Catholics.

Think about that number for a moment, 92 percent, and put it in the context of what I presume most know about how badly divided the American Catholic Church is on virtually everything. The truth is that if we had a representative sample of 100 American Catholics, I doubt you could get 92 of them to agree on the day of the week. On the left there would be some crowd suspecting a hierarchical plot to control our sense of time and on the right you would find a couple of grumpy guys who think we should still be using the Julian calendar. That is just the practical reality of it.

In that context, the fact the Pope has a 92 percent approval rating is nothing short of miraculous. Frankly, when we get around to the beatification and canonisation of Jorge Mario Bergoglio I think this could count as the first miracle.

And consider all the magazine covers the Pope has been on. He has been *Time* Person of the Year, and on the cover of *Rolling Stone* magazine. That is how you know you have arrived. But the first publication in the world to declare him Person of the Year actually was not *Time*. It was the Italian edition of *Vanity Fair*, not exactly a house organ of the Catholic Church. Three months into the game, it declared Pope Francis its Person of the Year.

Then there is the insight from that well-known Vatican expert, Elton John, who described Pope Francis as "a miracle of humility in an era of vanity".[15] It is a great line. I am waiting for the world to forget that Elton John said it so I can steal it.

There are many more examples of this Pope's popularity and it is fun to speculate, and 'soak in' the celebrity around Francis. But the real question is: what is beneath that celebrity? That is, is this just a pop culture phenomenon? Or is the world responding to something in Francis that is actually profoundly important and authentic and badly needed in our

---

[15] M.K. Haley, 'Sir Elton John says Pope Francis is "a miracle of humility"', *Catholic Herald*, 10 July 2013; accessed on 5 April 2016 at www.catholicherald.co.uk.

time? I would suggest the answer to the latter question is yes.

Which begs the issue of what it is the world is responding to. In attempting to lay that out, I begin with this assumption: there is a bizarre media phenomenon whereby sometimes the more cultural noise there is about a public figure, the less we actually know about them. You have to separate the wheat from the chaff. There are so many competing reconstructions and interpretations that it can be hard to know who the real person beneath the ferment actually is.

Three pillars to understanding Pope Francis

I will present three pillars to understanding who Francis is and what he is about. I submit two things in advance. The first is that if you understand these three things about Pope Francis, you will understand 90 percent of everything that he says and does. The second, which is a bit of a spoiler, is that these pillars are not only the keys to understanding the person of Pope Francis but they are also, in many ways, the mission statement for Catholic social services. The takeaway is that in Pope Francis you have, in effect, a Magna Carta for Catholic social services in flesh and bone.

The three pillars of Francis' identity, priorities and outlook are: one, a passion for the peripheries, both the geographic and existential peripheries of the world; two, a deeply missionary concept of Church; and three, mercy as the cornerstone spiritual message the world needs to hear from the Church at this moment in time.

A passion for the peripheries

Beginning with the passion for peripheries, we all know that popes often speak in gestures as much as in words. One category, one especially eloquent category of Pope Francis' gestures, is comprised of his trips. I have often said that, if you want to understand Pope Francis' view of the world, you do not need his spokesman, or a spin-doctor, all you need is his travel agent, because his trips will explain everything you need to know.

It is the furthest thing from an accident that Francis' first trip outside Rome as Pope, on 8 June 2013, was to Lampedusa, the island in the southern Mediterranean that is a primary point of arrival for impoverished migrants and refugees, generally from the Middle East and Africa, who are trying to make their way to Europe. The Pope went there to lay a wreath in the sea commemorating the 20,000 people who are believed to have lost their lives in the last two decades alone trying to make that very dangerous crossing over the Mediterranean.

That visit to Lampedusa was the first time Pope Francis rolled out what, in a sense, has become one of the standard rhetorical tropes of his papacy, the contrast between what he calls a "throw-away culture", in which whole categories of humanity are regarded as essentially disposable, versus what he describes as a "culture of encounter".

I know that, to Anglo-Saxon ears, the word 'encounter' may not have much pop and sizzle to it but in a Latin context, encounter is everything. It is about replacing this "throw-away culture" with a human environment in which people care for one another, not because of their utility to them but because of their inherent dignity and worth.

It is no accident that Pope Francis travelled to the Middle East, to Eastern Europe, to Asia and to Latin America before he went any place in the so-called First World. To date, he has only made one trip in Western Europe, a day trip to Strasbourg, to address the European Parliament. He still has not made a state visit anywhere in Western Europe. Pope Francis has made one visit to what we would recognise as the developed world, namely to the United States.

These are not accidents. In effect, this is the Gospel principle of "the last shall be first" as an actual, honest-to-God, program of governance.

Pope Francis' passion for the peripheries can also be seen in the way he makes cardinals. It is his tendency to bypass the traditional centres of power when he wants to create new cardinals, and that is the appropriate ecclesiastical verb. We say the Pope creates cardinals, which leads to the cynical old Roman joke that only God and the Pope can make something out of nothing.

In any event, when the Pope creates cardinals, he does not typically bestow these red hats in the traditional places. In the Italy of today, for example, it has escaped no-one's attention that Turin and Venice do not have cardinals but Agrigento in Sicily does and Ancona does. When Pope Francis decided to create the first ever cardinal in Haiti, he did not go to Port-au-Prince but went to the small Diocese of Les Cayes.

Looking around the globe, this is part of his program to try to lift up cardinals in places that have never had them. In the last consistory Tonga was given its first cardinal. You all probably knew that Tonga is a country but I did not until it was suddenly given a cardinal. It actually has a king and queen and is a place with a population of 100,000; it is like the city of Indianapolis, but the king and queen of 'Indianapolis' were there at the consistory and it was fantastic.

These are not accidents and these are not just PR gestures. This is a Pope who is leading us to embrace the marginalised, the forgotten, the isolated, the overlooked of the earth. That is the number one thing to understand about Pope Francis, his passion for the periphery.

A deeply missionary concept of Church

The second thing is Pope Francis' deeply missionary concept of Church. I have been covering popes for about 20 years and I have covered three: John Paul II, Benedict XVI and now Francis. If I had one iron-clad moral certainty on the back of those 20 years of experience about the papacy, it is that being Pope in our time is an impossible job. It is almost metaphysically impossible.

Think about what we want popes to be, and I do not mean the description of the office in the Catechism or in the Code of Canon Law. I mean the popular expectation, out in the streets. What do people expect from popes? We want them to be influential giants, conversant with all the great currents and the culture. We want them to be political titans able to wave a magic wand and make the world's problems disappear. We want them to be media rock stars. We want them to be *Fortune* 500 CEOs running a complex religious multi-national. And, of course, we want them to be living saints.

Any one of those things is hard to do as a life's work. Roll it up into one ball and it is a crushing burden. Go back and look at pictures of Karol Wojtyla in Krakow in October 1978 when he was elected to the papacy. Then look at images of him from the end, in April 2005. It was not just his age and it was not just the Parkinson's disease. It was the bone-crushing nature of this impossible burden.

What that means in practice is that every pope has to pick and choose. No pope can do all that is expected perfectly. The question is, when Francis has to pick and choose aspects of the job that are most important to him, where does he go?

I guarantee that, when Pope Francis gets out of bed in the morning, he does not fundamentally think of himself as an administrator or manager, even though managerial reform of the Church, beginning in the Vatican and radiating out, is an important part of the electoral mandate he was handed in March 2013, and he knows it is important. But it is not his top priority.

I guarantee that, when he gets out of bed in the morning, Pope Francis does not fundamentally think of himself as an intellectual, even though he is a very bright man. He does not aspire to be the Church's theologian-in-chief. That was Benedict XVI. That is where his energy went. That is not Francis.

Francis fundamentally thinks of himself as a missionary. Remember that when his priestly vocation was born, his original aspiration was to be Argentina's answer to Matteo Ricci and St Francis Xavier. His original dream was of being a missionary in China. Life did not have that in store for him but the embers of that missionary vocation continue to smoulder. They burn in the man's heart so that he is by every instinct, every fibre of his being, a missionary and he wants to preside over a missionary Church.

That is why one of Pope Francis' standard sound bites, the kind of thing he repeats over and over, is this invitation, or rather a kind of heartfelt plea, a *cri de coeur*, for the Church to get out of the sacristy and into the street.

Pope Francis is at his core a missionary. The most important document, if you want to read a document that gives a kind of hermeneutical key to unlocking his heart and mind, it really is not *Evangelii Gaudium* as sparkling a text as that is, and it is really not *Laudato Si'*, as complex and thoughtful as that is.[16] The key text, the base text for understanding Francis, is the 2007 document of the Latin American Bishops which they put together in Aparecida, at the famed Marian shrine, a text for which Jorge Mario Bergoglio of Buenos Aires was the lead author and chief editor.[17] It has at its core a call for a great continental mission. That is, this notion that the Church must break out, must shake off, must get past this reliance on structure and institutional prowess. We must realise that our 'cash value' in the era in which we live is not inside the sanctuary, it is not inside magnificent buildings, it is out in the street meeting people where they live. That is the key to understanding this Pope.

And as a missionary, there is an almost preternatural instinct of daring in this model. I would not use the word reckless to describe Francis' approach but, put it this way, if he were to be faced with a choice between caution and daring, daring would win every day of the week, and twice on Sunday.

There is an invitation to all of us implied in that to be daring ourselves, to be bold, to take risks, to move into unchartered waters. As John Paul II used to say, "Put out into the deep". And in his own way Francis is very much an advocate for that.

So that is the second point, this missionary perception of what the Church is all about, missionary as opposed to institutional, structural, political.

Mercy as the cornerstone spiritual message

The third pillar for understanding what this Pope is about is mercy as the spiritual 'Rosetta stone'. There is a great deal we can say about mercy,

---

[16] Pope Francis, 2013. Apostolic Exhortation: *Evangelii Gaudium* and Pope Francis, 2015. Encyclical Letter: *Laudato Si'*. Vatican City: Vatican; accessed on 5 April 2016 at w2.vatican.va.

[17] Consejo Episcopal Latinoamericano (CELAM), 2007. *General Conference of the Bishops of Latin American and the Caribbean Concluding Document*, 13-31 May. Aparecida, Brazil: CELAM.

which is literally this Pope's motto. The motto is the same one he had as the Archbishop of Buenos Aires and it is a Latin phrase that comes from a homily of the Venerable Bede about the Gospel scene of the call of Matthew. The line is *miserando atque elegendo*, which is a little hard to bring into English but basically means choosing through the eyes of mercy, making decisions on the basis of mercy.

We are living in the middle of a special jubilee Holy Year of Mercy called by Pope Francis which clearly flows from this invitation, this emphasis, this accent on mercy. His very first Sunday homily as Pope was not given in the magnificence of St Peter's Basilica but in St Anne's, the working parish church of the Vatican. It is where the worker bees, the guys who scrub the floors and open the mail and fix the lights and so forth, go to worship on a Sunday. In that homily, Pope Francis, speaking with no notes, said, "I hope that the theologians in this room will forgive me but in my opinion the strongest message of the Lord is mercy".

One of the places you can see this passion for mercy percolating in an especially palpable fashion in Pope Francis is his deep commitment to the sacrament of confession. You may know, for example, that during the Good Friday penitential service in the Vatican he hears confessions himself, which popes have done before. What he has added is that before he hears confessions, he confesses himself. He goes to another one of the priest confessors in the Basilica and receives the sacrament himself before he administers it. Further, this has now become a standard part of the itinerary for his parish visits.

The Pope is also the Bishop of the local Diocese of Rome. One of the ways popes try to express that is by getting around and making parish visits. There are 273 working parishes in Rome. No pope can get to all of them but they try to get to as many as they possibly can.

Francis made his first parish visit in May 2013. He went out to Saints Elizabeth and Zachary, which is the Prime Porta neighbourhood up in the northern part of town, a working class neighbourhood. I happen to know the pastor there, a Romanian immigrant by the name of Fr Benoni Ambarus. Everyone calls him Padre Ben. I called him up and said, "Listen, Padre Ben, do you mind if I come and hang out? I'd like to see the show". He said, "Sure".

The plan was the Pope was supposed to get there at 10.30 in the morning. At 9.30 I was sitting in Padre Ben's office and we were having coffee, 'shooting the breeze', and all of a sudden we heard the 'thump, thump, thump' of a helicopter in the distance.

And at first we thought it was the *carabinieri*, the Italian para-military police, doing a security flyover. But the sound of the chopper blades grew louder and louder and finally we realised it was the papal helicopter. The guy was showing up 45 minutes ahead of schedule.

So after I had run to grab the defibrillator to restart Padre Ben's heart, he sprinted out to the parking lot where they had set up a makeshift helipad. The papal chopper landed and Bergoglio, Pope Francis, popped out and said, "Hey, listen, sorry for the early start, but in addition to saying Mass and chatting to the people and all that, I would also like to hear some confessions".

It was not part of the program, so Padre Ben ran and grabbed eight people, basically completely at random, and said, "You are going to confession". I was standing there watching this and one guy looked up at Padre Ben and said, "Well, Father that's very sweet but I've been waiting here for three hours. I don't want to lose my spot in line to see the Pope". Padre Ben said, "Oh, trust me". So he brought eight people into the Church and lined them up in front of the confessional and one by one Pope Francis heard their sins and administered God's forgiveness.

Now catch the point. In part, this is just about Pope Francis trying to be a good Bishop of Rome and doing his pastoral duty. But if you want an insight into Pope Francis that you dare never forget, in five star, banner headline, full living colour, always bear in mind this about him: beneath that humble, simple, pastoral exterior, which is all real, by the way, lies the mind of a brilliant Jesuit politician. There are no accidents, there are no uncalculated moves. This is not 'Evening at the Improv' with Pope Francis. In this case he wanted the world to see the Pope making a point of celebrating the Church's premier rite of mercy.

On the papal plane in July 2013, when Pope Francis was returning from Brazil, he did the first of what have now become these legendary in-flight press conferences. And by the way, I travel with popes all the time and in many ways it is a dismal experience. We are stuck back in steerage, so the seats are uncomfortable and the food is generally mediocre but with Pope Francis, I will give it this, the in-flight entertainment is spectacular.

In that July 2013 press conference he said something that, with the benefit of hindsight, has become the mission statement of this papacy. We asked him a question about divorce and civilly remarried Catholics, which of course was one of the hot button issues of the 2014-2015 Synods of Bishops on the Family. He gave us an answer. But implied in that answer there is a paragraph that you really ought to look up, and I think it ought to be printed on t-shirts somewhere, in which the Pope says, "This time is a *kairos* of mercy", using that evocative Greek New Testament term that means a privileged moment in God's plan of salvation.[18]

This is a Pope who believes the providential logic for his election, the reason the Holy Spirit placed him on the throne of Peter, was to lift up, dust off and make resplendent once again the Church's message of mercy.

Pope Francis is a savvy Christian pastor. He understands that he has a responsibility to do two things: he must pronounce both God's judgement and God's mercy. One without the other would be falsification of the Christian message. But I think his calculation has been that so often the world has heard our judgement with crystal clarity and now it is time for them to hear and to see and to feel and to taste, and even to smell, our mercy.

If you ask me how Pope Francis will be remembered, I predict that it is not as a progressive revolutionary maverick reformer, Pope of the people, any of that stuff. I believe that, in the long run of history, we will remember Francis as the Pope of mercy.

Of course, that idea did not originate with him. Pope Francis is hardly the first figure in the Christian tradition to talk about mercy. It is a concept that goes all the way back to the very beginning. The death of

---

[18] Pope Francis, 2013. Press conference during the return flight from XXVIII World Youth Day in Rio de Janeiro, 28 July. Vatican City: Vatican; accessed on 5 April 2016 at w2.vatican.va.

God on the cross to redeem the world was the supreme act of mercy. But I believe Pope Francis will be the Pope who will be remembered as the one who made that message 'hear-able', who made that message 'see-able', who made that message 'feel-able' in his own time.

If you remember these three things about Francis, passion for the periphery, a deeply missionary concept of the Church and this emphasis on mercy, you will understand the man. And you will also understand why I tell you he is the Magna Carta in flesh and bone for the work of Catholic social services.

This program that I have described is fairly ambitious. It is easy to talk about mercy. It is easy to extol the peripheries and it is easy to pledge oneself to mission as a kind of life's blood. What is difficult, of course, is to translate that into practice. But it is a key agenda, figuring out that job description, that lofty inspiring vision about what the Church can be and what that means in the concrete details of what you do, day in and day out.

To make that a success you are going to need many qualities of heart and mind. You are going to need imagination. You are going to need perseverance. You are going to need patience. You are going to need a dialogic spirit. You are going to need all kinds of things. But I guarantee you that one quality, which has to be in the mix, one quality without which we cannot succeed in this endeavour, is a lively sense of humour. If you cannot occasionally laugh at the challenges that stand before you, laugh at the surreal nature of the situations in which you find yourself, that is a prescription for perpetual heartburn and the way madness lies.

A lively sense of humour in the Church

The good news is that you can find this lively sense of humour in the Church even in the most wildly improbable places. Back in April 2005, when Cardinal Joseph Ratzinger was elected to the papacy, that is Benedict XVI, I did one of these InstaBooks about the new Pope. It is called *The Rise of Benedict XVI*.[19] In the Vatican press corps there is a

---

[19] J.L. Allen Jr, 2005. *The Rise of Benedict XVI: The Inside Story of How the Pope was Elected and Where He Will Take the Catholic Church*. New York: Doubleday.

tradition that when one of us does a book about the pope, we inscribe a copy to the Holy Father and then we give it either to his press secretary or his spokesman or somebody who is interested.

To be honest, it had never occurred to me for a moment that popes actually read these books. In my mind's eye I envisioned a box in the basement of the Apostolic Palace where they all get tossed in and gather dust.

Benedict was elected in April, I wrote the book in May, and it came out on 1 June. I dutifully inscribed the copy and I gave it to Joaquín Navarro-Valls, who at the time was the Pope's spokesman. And then I forgot about it.

Fast forward to August 2005, my wife and I were back in the States. We were visiting my then 93-year-old grandmother, who lived out where I grew up, which is in the rural west of Kansas.

To be precise she lived in a place called Hill City, which is my candidate for the worst place name in America because there is no hill and there sure as hell is no city. We are talking about 600 people on a good day. The only time basically anybody ever visits Hill City is during the fall, because that is pheasant hunting season.

I have travelled the world fairly widely and I have stayed in some pretty funky lodgings on God's green earth but just to give you a sense of the cultural milieu of Hill City, America, there is one 11-room motel which is the only place I have ever stayed where there is a laminated sign in the bathroom that reads, "Please do not gut your birds in the sink".

There we were in Hill City, America and my cell phone went off and Navarro-Valls was on the other end of the line. He said to me, "Hey John, I wanted you to know that I'm with the Holy Father". Benedict was vacationing at that point in Northern Italy, in Valle d'Aosta, staying in a Salesian chalet. Navarro-Valls continued, "I wanted you to know he came down to breakfast this morning with your book in his hands and he had a message that he asked me to pass on".

Now, if you have just been told that the Pope has a personal reaction to something you have written about him, you want to make sure your tray table is in the full upright and locked position, because the skies may get a little bumpy. I said, "Of course. That's great. What's the message?"

To understand this you need to know that my book is divided into thirds. The first part was the final days of John Paul II, the middle part was the inside story of how Cardinal Ratzinger had been elected as Benedict, and then the third was my projections for where things would go.

So Navarro-Valls said, "The Holy Father's message is the following: 'Please thank Herr Dr Allen for having written this book, particularly the last part about the future of my papacy because it has saved me the trouble of thinking about it for myself'".

I like to think he was kidding. I would suggest that on this score, as on so many others, we take our cue from the Holy Father. If we can take an unblinking, utterly realistic look at the depths and the challenges that the broken, bruised and hurting world sets before us, the seeming impossibility of administering the medicine of mercy in a culture where, and at a time when, mercy seems to be in increasingly short supply, if we can look at all of that with eyes wide open, but we can do it with a twinkle in our eye rather than despair in our hearts, or bile in our spleens, then that, I would suggest, is a winning strategy for Catholic social services in the early 21st century.

If you are ever tempted to lose your sense of humour, remember that great line from Hilaire Belloc, the late 19th-early 20th century, Anglo-French writer, "wherever the Catholic sun doth shine, there's laughter and good red wine. At least I have always found it so. *Benedicamus Domino*!"

Mission Making a Difference in a Changing World

Maria Harries with Jayne Lloyd, Al Curtain,
Deb Tsorbaris and John Falzon

On 25 February 2016, a forum was held as part of the Catholic Social Service conference, *Review, Re-imagine, Renew: Mission making a difference in a changing world*. The forum, which I chaired, included four presenters who shared their insights on the topic 'Mission Making a Difference in a Changing World'. The four presenters were:

- Jayne Lloyd, Chief Executive Officer of CatholicCare in the Northern Territory,
- Al Curtain, Board member of MacKillop Family Services,
- Deb Tsorbaris, Chief Executive Officer of the Centre for Excellence in Child and Family Welfare, and
- Dr John Falzon, Chief Executive Officer of the St Vincent de Paul Society National Council.[20]

Introduction

Mission making a difference? Without costly and exacting data, it is not possible to provide an empirically precise and evidence-based set of facts on how mission makes a difference. Nor might any of us think it useful to develop such data. So, the challenge facing these presenters was an interesting one. What does Catholic Social Teaching tell us? What is it that makes a difference to those we serve? What does it look like? Why is it important? And how do we know who thinks it is important or what it is that makes a difference? These questions are particularly interesting

---

[20] For information on CatholicCare NT, MacKillop Family Services, the Centre for Excellence in Child and Family Welfare, and the St Vincent de Paul Society, see respectively www.catholiccarent.org.au, www.mackillop.org.au, www.cfecfw.asn.au, and www.vinnies.org.au; accessed on 14 May 2016.

in an environment in which outcomes have become the singular measure of service success about how we make a difference.

All of us are aware of the significance of relationships and values in our work and we accept they make a difference to how we work, with whom we work and how we grow our own capacities to work in tough environments. What these presenters were invited to do was to contemplate the missionary concept of the Church and consider the importance of the nature and location of mission, not just within a changing world but also within a world of increasing inequality and turmoil in which we must articulate our mission values. Fundamental to the arguments of these presenters is how we understand the Catholic way that we do things and the Gospel values that drive us.

A summary of each of the presenters' main points is provided below.

Jayne Lloyd

Talking about CatholicCare in the Northern Territory is one of my favourite things to do. For us, trying to make a difference in the way that we do our work is critical. So it is not just about the outcome, it is also about how we get there. In practical terms, we are a missionary organisation and a missionary diocese in that we cover a vast area. We have offices all over the Northern Territory including in very small Indigenous communities. In order to cover this vast area we have a couple of hundred staff delivering services.

One of the challenges in doing this work is how you maintain a culture that is very much aligned with the mission and Catholic tradition. That is something that we as an organisation have worked really hard to understand and in which to invest. To assist this, we have a mission facilitator on staff whose specific role is to look after mission and culture. We have had a position like this for around 10 years, so it is not new for us. Mission is integrated into our core work. It is not an add-on or something we cover just at orientation; it involves formation that happens all the time with our staff; it is ongoing.

When we look at our strategic directions statement, it is not a visionary document that is about growth, energy or domination in the Northern Territory; it is really about how we can do our work. It includes things like leadership and culture. We have 13 offices throughout the Northern Territory because we believe we need to be where the people are. So we do not fly in and fly out, or drive in and drive out. We invest in staffing infrastructure that is there among the people. We are constantly investing in an emerging workforce and building up a staff of local people who can serve their own community. We invest in partnerships and we dialogue with people in the communities and all of the stakeholders in a way that talks to who we are as a Catholic organisation.

When reflecting on the many things that have happened in Indigenous communities, like long-term disadvantage and the interventions, I think for us, with our Catholic identity and conditions, we offer a sense of certainty. We commit to a community. We have a Reconciliation Action Plan that really talks to how we engage with Aboriginal people and our Aboriginal staff. You can become very complacent with clients, the majority of whom are Indigenous, and when you have a lot of Indigenous staff, you can feel satisfied that you are doing enough. So we are constantly looking at how to increase the level of Indigenous leadership in our organisation. How do we honour what our clients and communities bring?

And I think that our experience with community shapes who we are and this adds to our identity. It builds on our own culture and mission, into which it is integrated. So hopefully we model mission in the way that we do business and the way we carry out our everyday work. We try to make mission part of the living culture of our organisation. Mission is really integral to who we are and how we do it.

Al Curtain

When asked to reflect on mission and the Catholic social services that we offer, the opening prayer of the Catholic Social Services conference provided moment to pause: "Strengthen our commitment to the common good, in the spirit of St Mary MacKillop who made a life-giving difference to so many". It is an honour to be part of such an amazing organisation as MacKillop Family Services, whose role is to carry forward this important work in the spirit of Mary MacKillop. With this in mind, I believe, in order for us to understand the importance of mission and the Catholic social services we offer, there are three pillars:

- As leaders we need to have a lived experience of prayer and meditation, an understanding of mindfulness, a practice of our faith and a unique insight into the mystery of the Eucharist in our lives. This is so important. The Eucharist is central to our Catholic faith. It is a profound personal and communal encounter, a very unique gift. I honestly believe that the power of the Eucharist, the importance of prayer or meditation, or some sort of spiritual discernment is very important to our Catholic identity as leaders involved in mission-oriented work.

- The second pillar comes directly from the principles of Catholic Social Teaching. When put into practice, it is incredibly profound; it is called 'See, Judge, Act'. I spent a few years in the seminary and studied the work of Cardinal Joseph Cardijn, the founder of the Young Christian Workers (YCW).[21] Cardijn explained very clearly the importance of See, Judge, Act, which can be understood as reflection, analysis and action. The important step though is the action. We really only learn if we take a risk and take action. It is not enough to simply review, reflect and analyse without that crucial step of action.

- The final pillar that is vitally important in the connection of mission with the Catholic social services we offer is what I call consistent, positive role models. As leaders we are all called to be positive role models for those who are marginalised, to be a voice for the voiceless and literally to stand with and for those who are so disadvantaged, the forgotten and the vulnerable. Who are the consistent positive role models for

---

[21] For information on the 'See Judge Act' model, see www.ycw.org.au/seejudgeact.php; accessed on 30 May 2016.

us? Where are they? For me, it is the Sisters of St Joseph, my foster parents and so many amazing leaders who have supported, challenged and encouraged me over so many years. We also know that we have the primordial role model in Jesus and the ongoing narrative of his life, death and resurrection as told to us time and again in the Gospel. Take a moment to pause now and reflect on who those consistent positive role models are for you as leaders. We all need them. They are there. We just need to take the time to reflect intentionally on who these people are and how important they are to us. Then we need to tell them that.

By integrating these three pillars into our lives and our work as leaders we really can review, renew and re-imagine our mission in the world to stand in solidarity with the poor.

Deb Tsorbaris

I would like to share some reflections on my own working life so far, and on some key issues that affect children and what lies ahead.

Our mission as a peak body, at the Centre for Excellence in Child and Family Welfare, is for Victorian children, young people and families to be safe, happy and connected and to get the support they need when they need it. We were established by a group of female philanthropists about 103 years ago and have been tireless in advocating for children ever since. In those early days, times were very different. The 1911 Census indicated that there were 4.5 million people in Australia, the median age was 24 years and only four percent of the population was aged over 65 years. Around the middle of the 19th century, the infant mortality rate was about 125 deaths per 1,000. Women did not get the vote until 1902 and Aboriginal people were not given the right to vote until 1962. I say these things by way of understanding who we were and then we can figure out who we are now.

It was 30 years ago that I completed two qualifications in nursing. However, the working environment I am in now bears no resemblance to what it was then. Today we have funding service agreements, accreditation, regulation, datasets, social networks, royal commissions, NDIS (National Disability Insurance Scheme) and the list goes on. It feels very different. And while we are interested in children's wellbeing, not all children are thriving as they should. One in 30 children still goes to bed and to school hungry. There is a huge surge in reports to child protection authorities, nearly 100,000 a year. One in four Australian students failed to complete secondary school and we still have 197 children in detention. The debate around gender equality for women continues. In terms of wage disparity, women are still earning around 25 percent less than their male counterparts doing the same work.

So where do we need to focus? We need to be proactive and be prepared to adapt and change. We must be more family-directed and really consider that families come in many forms. We understand now, particularly in the funded sector, that we are actually the designers of the system; it is no longer the government alone. Today, in the sector, there are professionals and non-professionals alike and we need to acknowledge the wonderful work that gets done in the community. Critical to our reflection is the Royal Commission into Institutional Responses to Child Sexual Abuse. We are, rightly, very sad about our past, we must make redress, and we must make sure those things do not happen again.

We need to get used to the changing world that we are living in, in particular the social and digital age. And we must work together. It is not always the case in community social services that we do this.

There are many and varied ways of activism. Look at Rosie Batty's selflessness and honesty[22] and some of the innovations that young people are exploring; the traditional ways of doing advocacy are not necessarily going to cut it any more. We really need to think within our communities, within our faith communities, how we might be inspired by this in our own work. We have to remain authentic and think about the incongruences in the way we think and in the way we work. We need to admit when we are wrong.

There is incredible leadership in our sector, and particularly within the faith community. I have mostly worked in faith-based organisations

---

[22] For information on Rosie Batty and the Luke Batty Foundation, see www.neveralone.com.au; accessed on 14 May 2016.

and am proud to say so. I grew up learning from many of those leaders. There are still many serious challenges ahead and we know what they are, and there is some urgency about dealing with them. We need to move ahead with courage and grace.

Dr John Falzon

I would like to begin with a story. I suffer from a particular affliction; I am directionally challenged. I get lost in most places but it gives me an opportunity to speak to strangers.

On one occasion in Parliament House last year I was standing in front of a lift and the security man could see I was lost. He offered to take me to the room that I was seeking and, while we were standing in the lift chatting away, he saw that I was from the St Vincent de Paul Society. He says, "Come here! Let me give you a hug. Thank you so much". The security guard then told me his story. He had been in a bad place and had gone to Wollongong for a job interview. He did not have any money to get home or to buy food, and had been wondering to whom he would go for help. He said, "It was actually the Salvos, but you don't mind do you?" I said I did not, but it was a beautiful story all the same. A couple of weeks later I had lunch with the then National Secretary of the Salvation Army and shared this story with him. He told me that the same security guard had given him an envelope with $20 for the Salvation Army crew who had helped him in Wollongong.

This story strikes me as prophetic. It tells me that the people about whom Pope Francis talks, those who are excluded by the market economy, by market idolatry, by capital systems that promise everything and deliver nothing, when given a little step up, do not wait to give. This bloke did not wait until he was more financially secure. He wanted to give what happened to be a fairly significant proportion of his income so that others could be helped. That just blows me away and I keep coming back to the beautiful line from the Scriptures: "The stone that the builders rejected has become the cornerstone" (*Matthew* 21:42).

So we have to ask ourselves: Who or what is our cornerstone? Is it wealth or power? Is it institutional privilege? Is it our position as a so-called helping profession? Is it political positioning?

Jesus is, of course, the Biblical cornerstone, but what does this mean in our society if it does not extend to the people who have been pushed to the margins? If it is not the crushed and the weak, the shattered and the shunned, the excluded and the exploited, then what is our purpose? For whom are we here and how do we identify ourselves? To whom do we listen and are we going to listen? Who are we going to believe? From whom are we going to learn? The privileged and preferred, or the silenced and unheard? Who are the ones who are going to play the chief role for us in defining our mission and our purpose?

If we seriously want to change society and re-order it according to the radical logic of the Beatitudes, which turns everything upside down, then this will not be achieved by making the *status quo* our cornerstone. Rather, it is going to the stone that the builders, that is our society, reject. We will never achieve such change by asking politely, by begging for concessions or by being grateful for the crumbs that fall from the table of the powerful. If we are true to that message, it is time that we actually think and act as revolutionaries. But in the beautiful words of the poet Audre Lorde: "The true focus of revolutionary change is never merely the oppressive situations from which we need to escape, but rather that piece of the oppressor that is planted deep within each of us". This is an incredible challenge. We will only achieve liberation for ourselves if we fight for the liberation of others. We will never achieve our own liberation if we ignore those who are in chains. Their struggle is our struggle.

At the conclusion of the panellists' presentations, the session was opened up for questions and responses. The ensuing discussion built on the initial presentations in considering the issues of the impact of Government funding, striking an appropriate balance between prevention and response, and inspiring young people to focus on mission rather than fame and riches.

Impact of Government funding

Most of Catholic social services are reliant on government money. How do we balance the conditions of government that can be put on us with the Gospel requirement to be prophetic?

Panel members were unanimous in their view that such a balance can be achieved, but that it requires a clear focus on what is our core purpose, and the courage to speak out where that is needed.

John Falzon summarised this view: "We live in a real world, in a world of compromises and we need to make practical decisions. We need to look for the means to deliver our services and to fulfil our mission ... but if we are making the choice to self-censor, or to allow ourselves to be forcibly censored and silenced, then we are betraying the people with whom we have a sacred obligation to stand in solidarity". Deb Tsorbaris put this another way: "The most important thing is that we actually question the requirements that might be imposed on us. If we are not going to do it, nobody else will".

Jayne Lloyd's reflection resonated with the panel and the conference: "It is the work we do that gives us credibility and gives us a voice so that we can influence policy".

Why not focus on the underlying factors that lead us to the problems we have?

Panel members agreed that our focus should be on prevention; that it does happen, but that Governments and communities do not adequately invest in work with families and children, which we know can prevent many of the problems that require social services and attract funding. It is a challenge to us to change this focus.

Underlying factors extended to basic issues such as domestic violence and homelessness and housing stress. Both are fundamental; both are areas where we can make a huge difference. Funding is needed, but so is cultural change across the society. It is part of our prophetic calling to lead such change!

How can we help inspire students to go on to work with the passion we hear in you, to divert them from 'I want to be rich and famous'? (a question posed by a pastoral associate at a large secondary college)

Panel members readily acknowledged the depth of this challenge. They identified some essential elements in offering inspiration: leading by example, exuding the hope that inspires us, and engendering political reflection.

Al Curtain put flesh on those bones, and built on his earlier comments about the centrality of 'See, Judge, Act': "Look at the two Young Australians of the Year who did the laundry service around Australia.[23] That is just incredible. I would be saying to young people, here are some really good inspiring stories of what is happening now. So we are talking about positive role models. Who are the people out there doing inspiring things? And what do they want? Where do they see themselves in five years, in 10 years, beyond this digital age? That consistent positive message is really important for me. The faith perspective is great too; it is foundational for me".

Conclusion

The four presenters met the challenge of outlining how mission makes a difference in their services. The inspirational Fr Gerard Hughes SJ, who died in 2014 and is perhaps best known for his wonderful book, *God of Surprises*,[24] said that he sought God in the turmoil rather than in the tranquillity. The presenters have provided us with enchanting insights into how they have found and follow the mission of Jesus amidst the turmoil of design and delivery in Catholic social services across Australia. They each 'see' the complexity, the pain and the challenges facing contemporary humanity and have emphasised their different applications. Their appreciation of the plight of the people 'at the periphery' would provide soul food for Pope Francis, whose prophetic voice about accompanying those who struggle, is such a gift to us all in social services.

The presenters pay particular attention to the urgent needs of our Indigenous peoples and their communities as well as vulnerable children and adults and the victims of the scourges of sexual abuse and family violence. More broadly, they highlight key elements of their works that remind us all of the gifts we have in our midst in Catholic social services as

---

[23] In 2014 Nic Marchesi and Lucas Patchett founded Orange Sky Laundry, a free mobile laundry in an old van, to assist the homeless. Since then, the world-first idea has expanded to five vans in Brisbane, the Gold Coast, Melbourne, south-east Victoria and Sydney and involves over 270 volunteers; accessed on 30 May 2016 at www.australianoftheyear.org.au/.

[24] G.W. Hughes, 2008. *God of Surprises*, revised and updated edition. London: Darton, Longman and Todd Ltd.

we 'judge' what to do and decide how to 'act': the visionary and enduring fundamentals of Catholic Social Teaching; our history of activism for the most vulnerable; the long-lasting leadership of the women and men of faith who remain our role models; and the need to lead with courage and to face the hostility from those who demand that we sacrifice vulnerable people in order to satisfy managerial orthodoxies.

Some of us may indeed be 'geographically challenged'. However, it is clear that our services are in the hands of leaders whose devotion, sense of the spiritual, belief in the fellowship of Jesus and relentless works of activism are unquestionably directional. So importantly, these four leaders have highlighted that in order to care for those we accompany in their distress we need also to accompany each other, develop our skills, support our colleagues, develop our ministries and liberate ourselves to pursue the fight for others as we make sure that mission makes a difference.

Pope Francis, Catholic Social Teaching and the Right to Migrate

Frank Brennan SJ

Forty-one years a Jesuit, I had never met a pope. Back in 1986, I was adviser to the Australian Catholic Bishops on Aboriginal land rights. Pope John Paul II came to Alice Springs, met with Aborigines and Torres Strait Islanders, and spoke strongly about the rights of Aborigines to retain title to their traditional lands. Next day, Archbishop John Bathersby told me the amusing story that the Pope had arrived at Alice Springs airport where he had mistaken Wagga Wagga's Bishop William Brennan for me. Bishop Brennan was very gracious about the matter when we embraced during the sign of peace at Mass. Some years later I did some work for the Pontifical Commission for Justice and Peace in Rome. After one meeting the President, Cardinal Roger Etchegaray, invited me to stay in Rome and to concelebrate Mass with the Holy Father at a major event in St Peter's Square the following Sunday. I did not see any reason to change my Saturday flight. As I sat on the floor to celebrate Mass with the staff of the Jesuit Refugee Service in Bangkok that Sunday morning, I told them that I knew where I would prefer to be.

On arrival in Rome in January 2016 to prepare for the Global Foundation's roundtable on 'Rejecting the "globalisation of indifference" – mobilising for a more inclusive and sustainable global economy',[25] the Australian Ambassador to the Holy See, John McCarthy QC, asked if I would like to meet the Pope. Without the slightest hesitation, I said I would. The ambassador organised a ticket for me to attend the regular Wednesday papal audience with thousands of other pilgrims. But he assured me I would be in the front row with a good chance of meeting my Jesuit colleague with the name 'Francis'.

The audience was due to commence at 10am. I arrived about twenty

---

[25] For details of the roundtable, see www.globalfoundation.org.au/#!global-governance/bqftr; accessed on 24 April 2016.

minutes early. The Pope was already working the room, moving through the crowd towards his white upholstered throne. By 9.45am, he was ensconced, painstakingly reading his initial catechesis for the Year of Mercy. He finished his delivery by 10.05am. I spared a thought for the pilgrims who were arriving just on time. Then followed half an hour of Monsignori reading translations of the Pope's remarks in various languages. By 10.45am the Pope had then greeted the bishops and monsignori on stage who had gathered for their photo opportunities. The Pope started descending the stairs and I thought the event rather underwhelming.

But Francis did not beat any prompt exit. He spent the next 45 minutes greeting every individual in the bay immediately in front of me. There were about 200 people there. As far as I could judge, you had to be confined to a wheelchair, or a child with a life threatening illness, or a carer to be eligible for admission to that privileged space. I was completely overcome. Here was a Pope living out everything he says, and doing it right under my nose. He is the very embodiment of empathy, compassion and mercy. He has often delighted in quoting Francis of Assisi, "Preach the Gospel always and, if necessary, use words". The words had been spoken from the throne; now he was in real preaching mode with the people, especially the poor and the suffering. Mothers wept as they embraced him. Kids played games and offered him gifts. People in wheelchairs extended every limb they could to reach him. He was totally present to each of them, oblivious of the cameras and mobile phones except when kids asked him to pose for a selfie. Here is a Pope who embodies and enacts what he says about love and mercy. I later got to meet him briefly, but that is another story.

Another penny dropped for me with Pope Francis when I heard some of the criticisms of his visit to the Greek island of Lesbos and his bringing 12 Muslim asylum seekers home with him to the Vatican in April 2016. One letter writer wrote to *The Australian*: "As the Jesuits have always done, Pope Francis plays us for fools".[26] No, he does not; and neither do we. We Jesuits are guided by our founder Ignatius Loyola who treated everyone, including his enemies, as open to conversion and

---

[26] J. Turley, 'Upset with Pope', *The Australian*, 19 April 2016.

change. Introducing his *Spiritual Exercises*, Ignatius insisted, "A favourable interpretation should always be given to the other's statement. If misinterpretation seems possible, it should be cleared up with Christian understanding. So, too, if actual error seems to be held, the best possible interpretation should be presented so that a more correct understanding might develop". This insight helps us to understand why Francis washes Muslim feet and why he takes Muslim asylum seekers home on his plane. Through sacramental action and symbolic stands in solidarity, he is opening an intelligent conversation about inter-religious dialogue, migration and the rights of asylum seekers; he is not treating any of his listeners or onlookers as fools. He is inviting everyone to an encounter at the borders of life.

As Pope, or as the Bishop of Rome as he often prefers to describe himself, Francis is not prescribing answers or handing down definitive teachings to underlings, treating them as lesser intellects or as fools. He has the humility not to put himself in the same class of theologian as his predecessor Benedict XVI. He does not even claim to match John Paul II. With his long pastoral experience in Argentina, he is always wanting to distinguish Catholic teaching from pastoral practice. This is abundantly clear in his two Apostolic Exhortations *Evangelii Gaudium* and *Amoris Laetitia*.[27] He believes in and proclaims a God who through Jesus is able to love without limit, and to extend mercy across all barriers. His papal teaching still claims to be an espousal of the truth including an accurate acknowledgement of the limits on human goodness. But it is ultimately the espousal of the truth about an all loving, all merciful God who acts in the world, mediated to the world by a broken Church and by sinful Christians graced with the capacity to respond to God's grace no matter what their own shortcomings.

His pastoral solicitude mixed with his unbounded faith in a merciful God allows him to proclaim, "Because of forms of conditioning and mitigating factors, it is possible that in an objective situation of sin – which may not be subjectively culpable, or fully such – a person can be living in God's grace, can love and can also grow in the life of grace and

---

[27] Pope Francis, 2013. Apostolic Exhortation: *Evangelii Gaudium* and Pope Francis, 2016. Post-Synodal Apostolic Exhortation: *Amoris Laetitia*. Vatican City: Vatican; accessed on 24 April 2016 at w2.vatican.va.

charity, while receiving the Church's help to this end". He is then able to note, "In certain cases, this can include the help of the sacraments", pointing out that "the Eucharist is not a prize for the perfect, but a powerful medicine and nourishment for the weak".[28] He espouses the place of the formed, informed conscience, urging us all to be true to such a conscience:

> We have long thought that simply by stressing doctrinal, bioethical and moral issues, without encouraging openness to grace, we were providing sufficient support to families, strengthening the marriage bond and giving meaning to marital life. We find it difficult to present marriage more as a dynamic path to personal development and fulfilment than as a lifelong burden. We also find it hard to make room for the consciences of the faithful, who very often respond as best they can to the Gospel amid their limitations, and are capable of carrying out their own discernment in complex situations. We have been called to form consciences, not to replace them.[29]

Just as we are called to act according to conscience in our personal relations, so too in our treatment of the stranger and the person in need. Both the personal and the political demand responses in good conscience.

This pope's first pastoral visit outside Rome was to Lampedusa, a small Italian island in the Mediterranean. Lampedusa continues to be a beacon for asylum seekers fleeing desperate situations in Africa and seeking admission into the European Union. Fleeing desperate situations in failed states like Somalia, asylum seekers transit another failed state, Libya, before boarding flimsy rafts in the Mediterranean Sea. It would be inhumane to send people back to Libya. Even before the recent outflow from Syria via Turkey, Lampedusa has been a lightning rod for European concerns about the security of borders in an increasingly globalised world where people as well as capital flow across porous borders. That is why Pope Francis went there. At Lampedusa on 8 July 2013, Pope Francis said:

> 'Where is your brother?' Who is responsible for this blood? In

---

[28] Ibid., *Amoris Laetitia*, Section 305 and footnote 351.
[29] Ibid., Section 37.

Spanish literature we have a comedy of Lope de Vega which tells how the people of the town of Fuente Ovejuna kill their governor because he is a tyrant. They do it in such a way that no one knows who the actual killer is. So when the royal judge asks: 'Who killed the governor?' they all reply: 'Fuente Ovejuna, sir'. Everybody and nobody! Today too, the question has to be asked: Who is responsible for the blood of these brothers and sisters of ours? Nobody! That is our answer: It isn't me; I don't have anything to do with it; it must be someone else, but certainly not me. Yet God is asking each of us: 'Where is the blood of your brother which cries out to me?' Today no one in our world feels responsible; we have lost a sense of responsibility for our brothers and sisters. We have fallen into the hypocrisy of the priest and the Levite whom Jesus described in the parable of the Good Samaritan: we see our brother half dead on the side of the road, and perhaps we say to ourselves: 'poor soul…!', and then go on our way. It's not our responsibility, and with that we feel reassured, assuaged. The culture of comfort, which makes us think only of ourselves, makes us insensitive to the cries of other people, makes us live in soap bubbles which, however lovely, are insubstantial; they offer a fleeting and empty illusion which results in indifference to others; indeed, it even leads to the globalization of indifference. In this globalized world, we have fallen into globalized indifference. We have become used to the suffering of others: it doesn't affect me; it doesn't concern me; it's none of my business!

Here we can think of Manzoni's character – 'the Unnamed'. The globalization of indifference makes us all 'unnamed', responsible, yet nameless and faceless.[30]

He makes the political personal; he casts the responsibility for the one in need on to the other who has the capacity to help directly as an individual, or indirectly as a citizen or legislator in a nation state able to open borders to the asylum seeker.

Another key insight into Francis was revealed when he addressed the United States Congress in September 2015. He commenced: "I am most grateful for your invitation to address this Joint Session of Congress in 'the land of the free and the home of the brave'. I would like to think

---

[30] Pope Francis, 2013. Homily at Lampedusa, 8 July. Vatican City: Vatican; accessed on 24 April 2016 at w2.vatican.va.

that the reason for this is that I too am a son of this great continent, from which we have all received so much and toward which we share a common responsibility".[31] He went in their door but only in order to bring them straight out his. He allowed his listeners to be lulled into the proud contentment of national identity before then turning the tables and establishing their shared geographic identity, underpinning their shared responsibility for the stranger and the one in need south of the Mexican border.

Though he does not write with the same clarity as his predecessors Benedict and John Paul, Francis has a more direct way of calling his listeners and interlocutors to account: to an account of conscience. He is a great one for the symbolic action in solidarity and for the folksy one-liner highlighting human interdependence.

When it comes to issues of migration, asylum and border protection, not even his predecessors can claim to have offered intellectual clarity about the limits of national responsibility. And that is because there is none. Francis has broken through some of the intellectual uncertainty with symbolic actions which speak to those on both sides of national borders, calling all to give an account of themselves, first with his visit to Lampedusa, then with his visit to the US-Mexico border, and recently with his visit to Lesbos in company with the two patriarchs, His Holiness Bartholomew, Ecumenical Patriarch of Constantinople, and His Beatitude Ieronymos, Archbishop of Athens and all Greece.

Not even John Paul II in his vast corpus of social encyclicals had much to say about the right to migrate. In his great human rights encyclical *Pacem in Terris* published in 1963, Pope John XXIII had spoken of the right to emigrate and immigrate. Harking back to Pius XII's 1952 Christmas message, John said:

> Again, every human being has the right to freedom of movement and of residence within the confines of his own State. When there are just reasons in favor of it, he must be permitted to emigrate to other countries and take up residence there. The fact that he is a citizen of a particular State does not deprive him of membership

---

[31] Pope Francis, 2015. Address to US Congress, 24 September. Vatican City: Vatican; accessed on 24 April 2016 at w2.vatican.va.

in the human family, nor of citizenship in that universal society, the common, world-wide fellowship of men.[32]

John went on to give his "public approval and commendation to every undertaking, founded on the principles of human solidarity or of Christian charity, which aims at relieving the distress of those who are compelled to emigrate from their own country to another".[33]

The UN's *International Covenant on Civil and Political Rights* (*ICCPR*) which was open for ratification just three years after *Pacem in Terris* made no mention of a right to emigrate. It confined its attention to the right to leave any country and the right to enter one's own country.[34] The Covenant added nothing of substance to the 1951 *Refugees Convention*[35] which did not accord asylum seekers the right to enter any country other than their own. That Convention simply ensured that any asylum seeker in direct flight from persecution was not to be disadvantaged for their illegal entry to a country were they successfully to gain entry, and that they were not to be refouled to their country of persecution prior to the determination of their refugee claim once they had gained entry, even if it be illegal.

---

[32] Pope John XXIII, 1963. Encyclical: *Pacem in Terris*, Section 25. Vatican City: Vatican; accessed on 24 April 2016 at w2.vatican.va.

[33] Ibid., Section 107.

[34] United Nations, 1966. *ICCPR*. Geneva: Office of the United Nations High Commissioner for Human Rights; accessed on 24 April 2016 at www.ohchr.org. Article 12 of the *ICCPR* provides:
1. Everyone lawfully within the territory of a State shall, within that territory, have the right to liberty of movement and freedom to choose his residence.
2. Everyone shall be free to leave any country, including his own.
3. The above-mentioned rights shall not be subject to any restrictions except those which are provided by law, are necessary to protect national security, public order (ordre public), public health or morals or the rights and freedoms of others, and are consistent with the other rights recognized in the present Covenant.
4. No one shall be arbitrarily deprived of the right to enter his own country.

Article 13 of the *ICCPR* provides:
An alien lawfully in the territory of a State Party to the present Covenant may be expelled therefrom only in pursuance of a decision reached in accordance with law and shall, except where compelling reasons of national security otherwise require, be allowed to submit the reasons against his expulsion and to have his case reviewed by, and be represented for the purpose before, the competent authority or a person or persons especially designated by the competent authority.

[35] United Nations, 1951. *Refugees Convention*. Geneva: Office of the United Nations High Commissioner for Refugees; accessed on 25 April 2016 at www.unhcr.org

Recent popes have wrestled with what constitutes a just reason for emigrating to another country not one's own and taking up residence there. While focusing on the individual and their human rights, the popes also give attention to the family, the community and the nation which are the privileged loci within which the individual enjoying their human rights is able to achieve their full human flourishing. Thus it is important to evaluate the national interest, especially when considering culture, religious freedom and economic prosperity. Though affirming the universal destination of goods and the universal brotherhood of man, the popes have tended to espouse national borders as necessary, contingent preconditions for full human flourishing. But in recent years, they have drawn attention to the particular responsibility which those behind secure national borders owe to those presenting at their borders seeking asylum in direct flight from persecution.

The popes know that the principles of Catholic Social Teaching they develop need to apply to a broad range of national borders. Some countries are net migration countries; others are not. Some net migration countries can control their borders, being able to allocate places for business, family reunion and humanitarian migration. There is no simple moral formula for determining what proportion of places should go to which categories, or for determining what percentage of national population growth should be accountable to migration rather than natural increase. Some migrant cohorts come from cultures and religious backgrounds similar to those in the nation state. Others are very diverse. Some countries insist that all workers be paid the same wages; others permit migrant workers from poor countries to be paid less, given that they will still be receiving much more than they would back home.

Paul VI, John Paul II, Benedict XVI and Francis have all addressed the United Nations. The last three popes have also addressed national legislatures. These addresses give them the opportunity to reflect on the role of civil law in fostering human flourishing. Benedict gave a particularly insightful address when he returned to his home country Germany and addressed the Bundestag. He asked the legislators, "How do we recognize what is right?" He answered, "In history, systems of law have almost always been based on religion: decisions regarding what was to be lawful among men were taken with reference to the divinity.

Unlike other great religions, Christianity has never proposed a revealed law to the State and to society, that is to say a juridical order derived from revelation. Instead, it has pointed to nature and reason as the true sources of law – and to the harmony of objective and subjective reason, which naturally presupposes that both spheres are rooted in the creative reason of God". Conceding the declining influence of Christianity, he nonetheless claimed that the encounter between Christianity and legislators in the west culminated after World War II in the commitment to "inviolable and inalienable human rights as the foundation of every human community, and of peace and justice in the world".[36]

All three recent popes have published an annual message for World Migration Day in addition to their annual message on the World Day of Peace. These addresses have required them to develop a fairly nuanced Catholic Social Teaching on migration. In 2001, Pope John Paul II warned against any indiscriminate licence to migrate and also against highly developed countries becoming too exclusive. He said:

> These rights are concretely employed in the concept of universal common good, which includes the whole family of peoples, beyond every nationalistic egoism. The right to emigrate must be considered in this context. The Church recognizes this right in every human person, in its dual aspect of the possibility to leave one's country and the possibility to enter another country to look for better conditions of life. Certainly, the exercise of such a right is to be regulated, because practicing it indiscriminately may do harm and be detrimental to the common good of the community that receives the migrant. Before the manifold interests that are interwoven side by side with the laws of the individual countries, it is necessary to have international norms that are capable of regulating everyone's rights, so as to prevent unilateral decisions that are harmful to the weakest.

> In this regard, in the Message for Migrants' Day of 1993, I called to mind that although it is true that highly developed countries are not always able to assimilate all those who emigrate, nonetheless it should be pointed out that the criterion for determining the level that can be sustained cannot be based solely on protecting their own prosperity,

---

[36] Pope Benedict XVI, 2011. Address to German Bundestag, 22 September. Vatican City: Vatican; accessed on 24 April 2016 at w2.vatican.va.

while failing to take into consideration the needs of persons who are tragically forced to ask for hospitality.[37]

In his World Day of Peace Message for 2001, John Paul II said, "The challenge is to combine the welcome due to every human being, especially when in need, with a reckoning of what is necessary for both the local inhabitants and the new arrivals to live a dignified and peaceful life".[38] John Paul II revisited the issue three years later in his 2004 Message for World Migration Day when he said:

> As regards immigrants and refugees, building conditions of peace means in practice being seriously committed to safeguarding first of all the right not to emigrate, that is, the right to live in peace and dignity in one's own country. By means of a farsighted local and national administration, more equitable trade and supportive international cooperation, it is possible for every country to guarantee its own population, in addition to freedom of expression and movement, the possibility to satisfy basic needs such as food, health care, work, housing and education; the frustration of these needs forces many into a position where their only option is to emigrate.

Equally, the right to emigrate exists. This right, Bl. John XXIII recalls in the Encyclical *Mater et Magistra*, is based on the universal destination of the goods of this world (cf. nn. 30 and 33). It is obviously the task of Governments to regulate the migratory flows with full respect for the dignity of the persons and for their families' needs, mindful of the requirements of the host societies. In this regard, international agreements already exist to protect would-be emigrants, as well as those who seek refuge or political asylum in another country. There is always room to improve these agreements.[39]

In his 2009 encyclical *Caritas in Veritate*, Pope Benedict XVI spoke about the "striking phenomenon" of migration (including the plight of lowly paid foreign workers), "a social phenomenon of epoch-making

---

[37] Pope John Paul II, 2001. Message for the 87th World Day of Migration, Section 3. Vatican City: Vatican; accessed on 24 April 2016 at w2.vatican.va.
[38] Pope John Paul II, 2001. World Day of Peace Message, Section 13. Vatican City: Vatican; accessed on 24 April 2016 at w2.vatican.va.
[39] Pope John Paul II, 2004. Message for the 90th World Day of Migrants and Refugees, Section 3. Vatican City: Vatican; accessed on 24 April 2016 at w2.vatican.va.

proportions that requires bold, forward-looking policies of international co-operation". He highlighted "the sheer numbers of people involved, the social, economic, political, cultural and religious problems it raises, and the dramatic challenges it poses to nations and the international community". He thought migration policies "should set out from close collaboration between the migrants' countries of origin and their countries of destination; [they] should be accompanied by adequate international norms able to coordinate different legislative systems with a view to safeguarding the needs and rights of individual migrants and their families, and at the same time, those of the host countries".[40]

Revisiting John Paul's 2001 Migration Day statement in 2011, Benedict added the observation: "States have the right to regulate migration flows and to defend their own frontiers, always guaranteeing the respect due to the dignity of each and every human person. Immigrants, moreover, have the duty to integrate into the host Country, respecting its laws and its national identity."[41]

Addressing the European Parliament in 2014, Pope Francis said:

> Likewise, there needs to be a united response to the question of migration. We cannot allow the Mediterranean to become a vast cemetery! The boats landing daily on the shores of Europe are filled with men and women who need acceptance and assistance. The absence of mutual support within the European Union runs the risk of encouraging particularistic solutions to the problem, solutions which fail to take into account the human dignity of immigrants, and thus contribute to slave labour and continuing social tensions. Europe will be able to confront the problems associated with immigration only if it is capable of clearly asserting its own cultural identity and enacting adequate legislation to protect the rights of European citizens and to ensure the acceptance of immigrants. Only if it is capable of adopting fair, courageous and realistic policies which can assist the countries of origin in their own social and political development and in their efforts to resolve internal conflicts – the principal cause of this phenomenon

---

[40] Pope Benedict XVI, 2009. Encyclical Letter: *Caritas in Veritate*, Section 62. Vatican City: Vatican; accessed on 24 April 2016 at w2.vatican.va.

[41] Pope Benedict XVI, 2011. Message for the 97th World Day of Migrants and Refugees. Vatican City: Vatican; accessed on 24 April 2016 at w2.vatican.va.

– rather than adopting policies motivated by self-interest, which increase and feed such conflicts. We need to take action against the causes and not only the effects.[42]

In his Message for the 2016 World Day for Migrants and Refugees, Francis made the observation:

> The presence of migrants and refugees seriously challenges the various societies which accept them. Those societies are faced with new situations which could create serious hardship unless they are suitably motivated, managed and regulated. How can we ensure that integration will become mutual enrichment, open up positive perspectives to communities, and prevent the danger of discrimination, racism, extreme nationalism or xenophobia?[43]

When he visited Lesbos in April 2016, he commenced with this concession: "The worries expressed by institutions and people, both in Greece and in other European countries, are understandable and legitimate".[44] He, like his predecessors, takes seriously the nation state's entitlement to maintain secure borders so as to enhance the prospects of full human flourishing for citizens seeking a full cultural, religious and economic life in harmony with their fellow citizens. But in a world with 60 million people displaced and seeking asylum, that is not the full picture, and thus not the entirety of Catholic Social Teaching on the right to migrate. Francis had already demonstrated in his address to the European Parliament that he understands the pressures on the modern nation state when dealing with migration flows. Thus his considered decision to go to Lesbos in company with the two patriarchs, not on a political mission but with a humanitarian purpose, drawing attention to the plight of those on the borders of life. Having acknowledged the understandable and legitimate concerns of those wanting to maintain secure borders, Francis went on to say:

> We must never forget, however, that migrants, rather than simply being a statistic, are first of all persons who have faces, names and

---

[42] Pope Francis, 2014. Address to European Parliament, 24 November. Vatican City: Vatican; accessed on 24 April 2016 at w2.vatican.va.
[43] Pope Francis, 2016. Message for the World Day of Migrants and Refugees. Vatican City: Vatican; accessed on 24 April 2016 at w2.vatican.va.
[44] Pope Francis, 2016. Address to People of Lesbos (Lesvos), 16 April. Vatican City: Vatican; accessed on 24 April 2016 at w2.vatican.va.

individual stories. Europe is the homeland of human rights, and whoever sets foot on European soil ought to sense this, and thus become more aware of the duty to respect and defend those rights. Unfortunately, some, including many infants, could not even make it to these shores: they died at sea, victims of unsafe and inhumane means of transport, prey to unscrupulous thugs.[45]

He then took 12 Muslim asylum seekers with him on his plane back to the Vatican. He made no pretence to tell European legislators how many asylum seekers they should accept, or how they should maintain the integrity of their borders. He could have decided to include some persecuted Christians in the cohort of 12, but he did not. He and the patriarchs issued a joint declaration espousing uncontroversial demands such as the need to address root causes of migration flows, and the need to do more co-operatively to help those in desperate need:

> [W]e call upon all political leaders to employ every means to ensure that individuals and communities, including Christians, remain in their homelands and enjoy the fundamental right to live in peace and security. A broader international consensus and an assistance programme are urgently needed to uphold the rule of law, to defend fundamental human rights in this unsustainable situation, to protect minorities, to combat human trafficking and smuggling, to eliminate unsafe routes, such as those through the Aegean and the entire Mediterranean, and to develop safe resettlement procedures.[46]

Catholic Social Teaching on the right to migrate provides us with principles which are useful in fostering a culture of engagement, seeking partial, more acceptable answers to insuperable problems. Pope Francis's symbolic actions, placing himself and his office deliberately at the borders of life, provides us with the incentive to develop a culture of encounter, animated to assist the asylum seeker who is perceived by us as 'other' but who is present and centre stage in the Pope's reflections. Francis, like his predecessors, is not proposing a borderless world but he is challenging his fellow Christians to display mercy and compassion across borders, and in dimensions they have dared not contemplate or attempt in the

---

[45] Ibid.
[46] Ecumenical Patriarch Bartholomew, Archbishop Ieronymos and Pope Francis, 2016. Joint Declaration at Lesbos (Lesvos), 16 April. Vatican City: Vatican; accessed on 24 April 2016 at w2.vatican.va.

past. He is not falling into the trap which John Finnis, the Oxford don and long-time member of the Pontifical Council for Justice and Peace and of the International Theological Commission, describes as clerical overreach producing "a rhetorical drift towards equating the borderless, cosmopolitan Church – in which there is 'neither Jew nor Greek' but all are equally and everywhere at home – with political community envisaged as if it likewise ought to be substantially borderless even if that resulted (but such consequences are not articulated even for consideration) in the annulling of national cultures, constitutions, and peoples".[47]

We are blessed that our recent popes have continued to espouse the basic human rights of the poor migrant worker and of the hapless asylum seeker while always maintaining a commitment to the political community's preconditions for contributing to the full human flourishing of those privileged to enjoy citizenship, especially in those nation states which boast the rule of law, economic resilience, and secure religious and cultural identities. The visits by Francis to Lampedusa, the US-Mexico border and Lesbos provide Australians of goodwill with the incentive and inspiration to revisit Catholic Social Teaching on migration and recommit themselves to the provision of asylum to those deserving it in our region while maintaining national security so that all who call Australia home might enjoy the benefits of their full human flourishing, including the capacity to help the neighbour in need. When answering who is our neighbour, we will then be more ready to respond to Jesus' answer in the mode of another question, "Which of these three, do you think, proved neighbour to the man who fell among the robbers?" The mature political community is the one which enables its members to respond, "The one who showed mercy on him" and to "go and do likewise" (*Luke* 10:36-7).

I must say, I am very pleased to have met Francis, though briefly, and we are blessed to have him appearing at the borders of life inviting us to respond with mercy. How would we feel if he were to turn up at Christmas Island, Nauru or Manus Island? And more to the point, what would we do in response to his challenge to us, a challenge grounded in the nuances of Catholic Social Teaching on the right to migrate?

---

[47] J. Finnis, 2011. 'Introduction', *Religion and Public Reasons*, Collected Essays, Volume V. Oxford: Oxford University Press, p. 12.

2016 Mary MacKillop Oration

Julian McMahon

Carte Blanche

I was given *carte blanche* to choose my topic for this Mary MacKillop Oration. It is usually easier to follow a given theme than it is to work out what your own topic is going to be. As the Oration was held during the 2016 Catholic Social Services conference and its theme was *Review, Re-imagine, Renew*,[48] the natural starting point for me to look for inspiration was to consider 'RE' words. As this was a Catholic event, the first 'RE' words that came to my mind were *resuscitate* and *reformation*. However, I thought that these may not be the best themes for such a talk so I moved to *respect*.

I spent some time researching respect in the context of the history of Western ideas and culture over the last 450 years. I thought that I would talk to you about the role and value of respect in this age when we all have to deal with so many complex situations that cross cultural and religious boundaries, where there is no real common education that we all share. It is much more difficult today to identify common cultural references, in the way that was once possible throughout history. Those who made decisions of state or led organisations 200 years ago would have had exposure to and been educated in common aspects of culture, would have shared very similar education, studying the same tried and true texts. This meant that one could assume there was a common understanding of particular cultural references. Today this is no longer the case.

I have thought for quite a long time that respect and courtesy are two words which apply in every situation we are faced with, regardless of the situation or with whom we are talking, whether it is with politicians

---

[48] The Catholic Social Services conference, *Review, Re-imagine, Renew: Mission making a difference in a changing world*, which inspired this volume, was held in Melbourne on 24-26 February 2016.

or the most marginalised and disadvantaged. Respect and courtesy are words which are universal and we all lose something when we do not have a common understanding of what they mean and seek to meet one another in relationship.

Well, I just gave that speech on respect in about one minute, so as important as respect is I realised that I needed a different topic for the Oration. To assist me in my preparation, I spoke with Cathy McGowan, Federal Member for Indi, whom I know and respect very much. As she was originally invited by the conference committee to deliver this Mary MacKillop Oration, I asked her what she had planned to talk about. Cathy knows a lot more about St Mary MacKillop and her work than I do. She was going to talk about Mary's work with the rural poor, the legacy of that commitment, and the heritage that provides for all who work alongside the poor and marginalised. I had thought maybe I would continue in that vein but I just do not have the knowledge about Mary MacKillop to do her work and her legacy justice.

Courage

One of the rules I have when I consider what to speak about on such occasions as this Oration is to put myself in the place of the audience where I would want to hear and be challenged by something worth listening to. So I am going to talk about something very serious and worthwhile, about courage, namely the courageous story of two Australians, Myuran Sukumaran and Andrew Chan, as they journeyed through their last days towards their executions. I hope to make it worth your while to be here tonight because much of what I am about to say is not known except to a very small number of people. So hopefully, this theme of courage, particularly in the face of injustice, will be worthwhile for us all.

Myuran Sukumaran and Andrew Chan were members of the Bali Nine who were convicted of trafficking drugs from Bali in 2005. Along with Lex Lasry, I became their lawyer in 2006. Myuran and Andrew were shot on Nusakambangan Island in the early hours of 29 April 2015. However, the first significant day in the irrevocable final lead up to their executions was 25 April 2015. Twenty-four hours before ANZAC

Day they were told that there was going to be an emergency meeting at Cilicap, a small city on the South coast of Java, from where one travels to Nusakambangan. Our team was very worried, knowing that this meant that a decision on their execution was possibly imminent. We travelled non-stop for 24 hours to reach Cilicap, arriving at precisely one o'clock on ANZAC Day at the Prosecutor's Office in Cilicap.

We went to the room where the meeting was just commencing. We had made it without even a minute to spare. There we were, two Australian consular officials, two Australian lawyers, the lawyers and diplomats for eight other prisoners, and about two dozen Indonesian officials. We sat at the table. I am unable to give a full account of this meeting at this time but needless to say that it was a significant moment in this long journey. One problem which was sprung on us was that some of the officials were saying that the two Australian prisoners were only allowed one lawyer between them; one lawyer per country was the theme. My colleague Veronica Haccou made the case for a lawyer for each client very quietly and firmly indeed, in both perfect Indonesian and English, and thankfully the ground shifted in our favour.

At the end of this meeting we had to go over to Nusakambangan Island, also known as Execution Island, notorious for its maximum security prisons. It is a small island, first used by the Dutch as a prison island. It now has seven prisons, and the ruins of old prisons too. It was here on this ANZAC day that the prisoners would be given 72 hours' notice of their execution. Many of you will know the events that took place in the lead up to this moment as we tried every possible way for this to be avoided. We had failed and it was now clear that this was the moment we were all dreading.

What happened in those 72 hours will stay with me always as I witnessed moments of extraordinary courage. We all went over to the prison island on a boat, and spent a long time at the prison reception. At the prison there were three or four times as many officials as usual. Finally, the process began; the first to be called were the Australians. There were four of us, the two consular officials and the two Australian lawyers, Veronica and me. We went into a room with 21 Indonesian officials. I recall counting them because it was so surreal. We were sitting at the front and the tables were set up so everyone was looking at us. Myuran was brought into the room in handcuffs. He was sat down.

It was coldly, or eerily, quiet. Our DFAT (Australian Department of Foreign Affairs and Trade) officer was on one side of Myuran and Veronica was on the other, I stood behind him. Lots of pictures were being taken; the Indonesians had a need constantly to document everything with pictures. The printer that was needed to produce the essential documents was refusing to work. We sat in silence for about 25 minutes while a group of people not suited to the task tried to fix the printer. Eventually it was fixed and the documents were printed.

The machinery of justice and death

Myuran could speak Indonesian fluently by this stage. The death warrant was read out. It was very long and took five or even ten minutes to be read out. It went through the whole procedural history of the case, the allegations, the verdicts, one court decision after another. I do not believe that anyone in the room thought the executions were necessary, not that they said anything to indicate this. They could not, they were officials, and they were just following orders to earn a living. What we were witnessing was the exercise of political power and the absence of political courage. I was thinking of the phrases "the machinery of justice, the machinery of death". I do not know where I first learnt these phrases but they are often in my mind. That day I was watching the machinery of death at work.

Myuran was very calm but he was strained. Strangely, as the whole warrant was read out, it did not include the many legal events of 2015. We had taken the case through four different courts over several months during that year. None of these were referenced in the document, meaning that the historical record did not actually include many of the legal steps taken. One of these events was the court application based on the apparent failure of the President to read the clemency documents relating to our clients. We had tried to get this apparent omission adjudicated before the courts but failed.

As these events were unfolding on this ANZAC Day we also had two legal processes still in progress. There was a Judicial Commission into corruption involving serious allegations relating to the time of the trial and appeals in 2006, before we Melbourne lawyers were involved. Our clients had sworn affidavits concerning those events, but the Judicial Commission had never spoken to them about it. There was also a case listed for a May hearing in the Constitutional Court. Legally this should have brought hope but the merits of our key legal positions were never actually determined. In reality, the machinery of justice and death was just rolling on and it was now apparently unstoppable.

Myuran sat and listened to this document as it was read out. He knew the truth of how the system really worked in Indonesia. He knew from his years in prison that justice could be up for sale and how it could be purchased. Indonesians themselves complain about this reality all the time. He knew about the power of the gangs and how they ran drugs in the prison. Over the years in prison Myuran had risen above it all. To rise above this injustice involves a lot of physical and moral courage.

Myuran was the most privileged prisoner in the jail because he had earned the right to be so. He acted with integrity, teaching and bringing in other teachers to educate the prisoners as part of their rehabilitation. The educational facility within the prison was completely safe, including for women, and free from crime. There were no drugs, no violence. He had risen above all of the bad things that were around him. Serious crime still came at him, every day, every week. It came to get into that space and take over. He walked around that prison with a handful of keys; such was the respect he had earned. It took a lot of physical courage to keep the place, his place, free. This freedom was his legacy to the prison. In a different way, mostly through Church activities and support from many friends, Andrew had carved out his own space, a vibrant religious, counselling and healing space desperately needed for so many prisoners.

I still do not quite have the words to describe the expression on Myuran's face while the death warrant was being read out. The words spoken to him said, "What a villain you are", yet Myuran believed that, if he had paid money at the right time to the right people, he would not be there. His eyes were watching a couple of people in the room who knew the whole story, the true story. The look on his face was a wise look with a quarter of a smile. It was the look of someone who was seeing his accusers in front of him and saying, "I don't hear you". He was saying, "You can't hurt me". He knew he was going to die but he had, in some way, risen above what was happening.

At the end of the reading, he was asked to sign the warrant of execution. The whole room, probably 25 people by then, sat expectantly as the document was handed to him for him to sign his own death warrant.

Speaking truth to power

At this point I remembered the expression I like to use where it is appropriate, and at this moment it could not have been more apt: "speaking truth to power". Myuran said he would not sign it because the document was wrong and untrue. Myuran's signature was essential on the document but he would not sign it. In that moment you could just see the machinery of justice falling into consternation because it did not know how to handle that. Everything froze.

This is a great example of speaking truth to power. To the men who were organising for him to be shot, his death was inevitable. It was definitely going to happen but, in the face of this, he said to the authorities, "Say what you like; I will insist on the truth at this moment". What he was saying was, "I will not lie. You're going to shoot me, but I will not lie. I will not sign your document unless it is true". As a way out of this impasse he was told that, if he wanted to say something for the record, the officials would type it into the document.

I suspect that the official who said that probably thought Myuran would speak one or two sentences and that would be that. To the officials' shock, he began the first of two memorable and beautiful speeches I heard that day. He delivered a speech declaring what was wrong with what was happening. He went through the reforms he had created while in prison, how many prisoners he had helped, re-educated and seen reformed; how he had fought off the drug gangs and had made part of the prison safe; how he was one of the handful of people in a prison of 1,000 who was working to see lives transformed. Myuran said it was wrong to kill someone like him who was doing so much good for other prisoners. I do not recall that he said as much but we all knew he was more than merely doing positive things; he was the leader of this good work.

He then said that if they included this truthful content in the death warrant he would sign it. That was a great and historical moment to witness. I had read about similar circumstances in other trials in the 20th century, but it was one of those stunning moments where Myuran, who did not necessarily have the education to know or understand quite what he was challenging, was demanding that the truth be known. The officials had to type it up and Veronica, whose Indonesian is perfect, insisted that it be completely accurate given the status of the document. So back and forth it went. It took some time before they got it right.

While that was happening, I recalled Myuran telling me that it was a pity all this was happening on ANZAC Day. Myuran had been feeling more and more connected to Australia as the months rolled on. He had reflected to me about reading and loving FitzSimons' book[49] on Gallipoli and that he was connecting deeply with the artist Albert Tucker and with Sidney Nolan's Ned Kelly paintings. He mused that he could see himself being someone like the artist John Olsen, if only he could live to be an old painter. Sometime later I saw his diary where, a few hours before he was given the message about the meeting on 25 April, he had written that he knew something like this was about to happen.

Eventually the document was done to the satisfaction of Myuran and Veronica. It was handed to Myuran and he signed it. Pursuant to that document, 81 hours later he would be shot.

Myuran was taken out of the room and Andrew Chan came in and he too was taken through the same process. To my pleasure, Andrew did exactly the same thing, and, although it sounded and seemed like it was organised, it was not. He said he was not going to sign his death warrant when it said things that were not true. By this time the officials were used to such a response from the Australians and the process worked a lot faster. Andrew gave the second powerful speech of the day, a very deeply

---

[49] P. FitzSimmons, 2014. *Gallipoli*. Milsons Point, NSW: Random House Australia.

moving account of his own rehabilitation, and how he had supported others in theirs. He said that Indonesia had rehabilitated him. Andrew was self-educated and his work in the prison as a minister of religion came from years of hard work and prayer. It was a speech that he had earned the right to say. His speech was also typed into the death warrant and he signed it.

These two men set a new, different benchmark that ANZAC Day. This is a truly historic example of speaking truth to power, saying to the people who are about to have you shot, that I will not go along with the deceit, concealing the real story; you have to listen to what I am going to say. The Indonesian justice system and its officials had to listen because they needed the men to sign the documents.

The human stories

There were many other examples in the last few days of the courage of these men and others in the face of injustice. About a day and a half before they were shot, in the Christian chapel, Andrew married Febyanti Herewila, a committed Christian whose life would be recognisable to many at the Oration. She is a pastor and was involved in a small school. She had been visiting the prison in Bali for a long time before she and Andrew became close friends. Over time they became deeply attached to each other. Until that last few weeks there was the hope that the men may have been pardoned and released. With the change of circumstances Andrew and Feby decided to get married. They had a joyous wedding with a small number of witnesses. It was a symbol of their deep love, a symbol of hope, and a symbol that they were refusing to be defeated.

There were eight people executed on 29 April 2015. One of them was Martin Anderson, a devout Muslim who was in jail for trafficking a very small amount of drugs. I had a precious encounter with him in his last few days. As I shared chocolate with him, he shared his story of how his faith and life of prayer were holding him together through what were to be his last days. He shared with me that he was happy because he had recently had vivid dreams of dying and being placed in his tomb. He saw the gates of Heaven welcoming him and he had a deep inner joy and confidence that he was going to go to Heaven after being shot.

Another personal story that touched me was Mary Jane Veloso, a young small Filipina prisoner who was also sentenced to death. Mary Jane was from a very poor family. Her own mother was there at the prison, and she had poverty written all over her. Mary Jane thought she was going to Malaysia, not Indonesia, to get a job in a new land. She arrived in Malaysia to be met with new plans and a ticket to Indonesia. Her suitcase had apparently been packed by other people who stashed drugs in it. It seemed more likely than not that she was innocent; she certainly said she was as did others involved in her case.

On the day of the executions, I sat next to her on the ground. She had her two children next to her, five- and ten-year-old boys. She held her five-year-old boy to whom we also gave chocolate. She encouraged her little boy to sing us a song in her dialect. I was watching her with him. She was whispering in his ear and he was singing and she was hugging him. As I watched her I could not believe that in an hour or less he was going to be taken away from her so she could be shot later that night. I was looking at a mother, looking at her son who was singing to me full of excitement and happiness. What I witnessed in that moment was the look of a healthy proud mother sharing her last few moments with her healthy beautiful son. When all the law and politics is forgotten, this scene confirms to me that capital punishment is wrong.

There was another prisoner's story that is just as confronting. Rodrigo was a Brazilian who was known to be suffering from a serious mental health condition. He did not understand that he was going to be executed. He had a beautiful cousin from Brazil present called Angelica who had sacrificed months of her life to look after him. There was also a wonderful local priest, Charlie Burrows, who journeyed with Rodrigo through these last days. It was only a couple of minutes before he died that Rodrigo finally understood, as he was being shackled to be killed, that he was going to be shot. Charlie was with him till the end.

I was not there to witness the executions. I was not allowed to witness Andrew and Myuran's last moments. Frankly, lawyers like me are not allowed to witness these things in most countries because of the possible political consequences for the powerful if we started talking about what we saw. Later that night, as it was drawing close to the execution, we were next to some of Mary Jane's family, sitting on the dock on the island, a few hundred metres from the killing field. We sat and waited for the inevitable.

The machinery of death won

This next account of events on Nusakambangan is based on what I heard from people who were there, including the pastors and priests who were with those about to be shot. The prisoners had just been taken out of the jail and driven to the location of the shooting. Our boys were leading the crowd of nine (it turned out later to be eight) who were going to be shot. As they left their cells, they were singing 'Amazing Grace', and they hugged all the guards. There was a chaplain with each of them: Christie Buckingham from Melbourne was with Myuran, David Soper, a life-long friend of the Chan family and chaplain, was with Andrew. They had all spent the last couple of hours praying. The whole caravan was driven to the killing field. They were talking to each other, consoling each other as their arms were strapped to two pieces of wood. They were singing and praying. Myuran said to Christie that he loved Indonesia, he forgave Indonesia and he wished good for Indonesia.

At 12.30am, twelve times eight, 96 rounds in total went off. They were shot. The machinery of death had won.

Two of Mary Jane's family were praying rosaries and when the shots rang out, so violently loud, they were howling with grief because their sister and cousin had just been shot. What they and we did not know until hours later was that Mary Jane had been pulled out of the line at the last minute. Apparently the prisoners worked out that she was not with them at the killing field after Andrew generated a roll call in the darkness. Mary Jane is not free, and there are still powerful people in Indonesia saying she must be killed but also powerful people in the Philippines working for justice. Her fate now hangs in the balance as a related case, concerning whether Mary Jane was duped into travel as a mule, works its way through the courts in the Philippines.

Heart and Head Together for Action

Julie Edwards

Introduction

In exploring this topic of reviewing, reimagining, renewing ourselves in order that our mission can make a difference in a changing world, I am going to draw from my own lived experience as a leader of a Jesuit organisation. At Jesuit Social Services we consciously draw on our Ignatian and Catholic roots to inspire, guide and sustain us and, as I explore this topic, the theme of the 2016 Catholic Social Services conference, I will be utilising a particular approach which in its simplest form can be summarised as 'heart and head together for action'.

Before I embark on this though I want to make a few comments. This paper is based on an address which had the benefit and the challenge of coming at the end of the conference so that I had heard what had gone before. As I listened during the conference I thought, well I am not going to be saying anything that has not already been said ... all good things, and I will not be saying anything different. Yet, I went home the night before I was to give my address just a little bit disturbed. I spent some time pondering that.

I liked everything I had heard. We seemed to be in furious agreement. We had all been talking about mission, about mission infusing all our activity, about how we must not succumb to being the arms and legs of government, how we have our own purpose and identity, about the poor, about community. Yet I had a nagging feeling; it did not quite ring true to me. There were fantastic people at the conference, from fantastic organisations ... family.

Yet I know that we are not all that we seem to be. I know this from experience and I know this because of what people at the conference said outside of the key sessions. I know that we do chase contracts for the purpose of growing our organisations. I have been at annual general meetings where the board chair has stood up and the first thing that came out of his mouth was announcing the organisation's success in exceeding the growth target.

I know that our organisations have gobbled up work, tendered successfully for services that meant Aboriginal organisations lost that work, putting them at risk of survival. I know that our organisations often do poor quality work, that at times we do not act as good parents to children in our care, or as respectful equals to those who seek our assistance, that at times people, families or communities are not left stronger as a result of their time with us, that we fail to speak out when we see things that are not in keeping with our Gospel values; think about prisoners and people seeking asylum.

I know that we have knowingly housed bullies or organisational sociopaths, that there is often a gap between our boards or management or staff in terms of understanding and implementing our mission, that we do not all invest our resources ethically or care for and live lightly on the earth that sustains us. I know these things. We are family.

Conference speakers Robert Fitzgerald and Maria Harries reminded us that we may have cleaned up our act regarding big issues such as sexual abuse. But what of our culture? Our leadership? Our governance? Do these **foster** or **constrain** an environment that lends itself to abuse, or lack of care, or to our not being whom we claim to be?

Another speaker, John Falzon, referred to the biblical quote: "The stone rejected by the builders has become the corner stone", and he challenged us to get close to those who are rejected. In whose interests are we acting? As I re-read that Gospel, it struck me that Jesus goes on to say immediately after that quote: "I tell you then that the kingdom of God will be taken from you and given to a people who will produce its fruit" (*Matthew* 21:42-43).

The kingdom of God will be taken from those who think they have the rights over the vineyard (maybe us) and given to a people who will produce its fruits (not necessarily us).

I suppose what I am saying is that we do not have a monopoly on goodness or virtue. Right now in this State, the Royal Commission into

Institutionalised Responses to Child Sexual Abuse is conducting its hearings. If ever there were a moment for us to stop, in all humility, and wonder if, beyond the rhetoric, we are producing the fruit of the kingdom of God, this is the time.

So when I come now to tease out a bit more of the approach I flagged at the outset, 'heart and head together for action', I want to do it with the sense of disturbance that I felt in my heart as I prepared to give the conference address.

Reviewing, reimagining and renewing ourselves?

As we all know, the task of reviewing, reimagining and renewing ourselves, personally and as organisations, is not a one-off event undertaken at a single point in time. It is the task of a lifetime. The major faith traditions understand this, of course, and assist us by building into each year seasons, for example, for review, atonement, renewal, rebirth.

As we all know, the Catholic Church marks the seasons of Advent, Christmas, Lent, Easter and other significant feast days, based on the understanding that we humans go on and off track regularly and need to be reminded about the fundamentals in life and faith.

But before we go off reviewing, reimagining and renewing ourselves and our organisations, we have some basics to attend to. The purpose of this reviewing, reimagining and renewing can be easily misunderstood or misinterpreted. It could amount simply to the development of new organisational visions or strategic plans, to growth strategies or business strategies. All well and good, but possibly nothing to do with our core purpose, our true identity.

Our reference point for any reviewing, reimagining, renewing must be our identity. Who are we? Why do we exist? What is our purpose? We need to get sharp clarity about these questions before we embark on reviewing, reimagining, renewing, or we risk shoring up or creating for ourselves a false identity.

And I would suggest that in this exercise of reviewing, reimagining, renewing ourselves and revisiting our identity, that we might benefit from changing the order to reimagining, then reviewing, then renewing.

In other words, we are not reviewing our identity as a static thing, but as a living thing that evolves in relationship to, and in the context of, our world, its people, its needs.

If we start down the track of reviewing our organisations in order to then reimagine and renew them, we run the risk of reviewing ourselves, our performance, in light of our existing understanding of ourselves. We are likely to ask such questions as, how are we performing against our strategic vision, our strategic plan? Or how do we measure up against our current understanding of our values? We are likely to limit or skew the scope of our review.

If, on the other hand, we start by reimagining ourselves, being very clear that we are not bound to any previous way of imagining ourselves, then possibilities open up. But how might we do this? What is needed for this to happen?

Heart and head together for action

Our starting point must be our *'heart'*: our lived experience, and the lived experience of others. Our focus must always be on the people we exist to serve. We do not exist to grow our organisations, to compete in the market of human service delivery. So we must be grounded in our relationship with others and our world, listening and learning. We should ask ourselves: what are my attitudes, behaviours? What is my heart telling me? To whom am I listening? Do I have the freedom to hear what they are saying? This is intimate and personal. It is not book knowledge. It is interior, felt knowledge.

'Head' is where we bring to the situation an understanding of our context, a reading of the signs of the times, using critical thinking and social analysis undertaken with intellectual rigour. This is a discipline. It is not the same as mouthing off and thinking we are social justice advocates; it means undertaking the disciplined work that allows us to deepen our understanding of the issue at hand.

St Ignatius of Loyola, founder of the Jesuits, said, "Always be mindful of the circumstances of place and person". And again comes the question, do we have the inner disposition to really see what these circumstances are, to see what the changing context is telling us?

'Together' means, in bringing our heart and head 'together', we enter into a process of reflection and discernment. This too is a discipline. Depending on the importance of the matter being considered, this can be a short or long exercise. It can range from being a simple sifting of feelings and thoughts, through to a thorough examination of all relevant components, of quiet and of conversation and of checking in again, beyond the rhetoric, on our lived values, attitudes, behaviours.

In this Ignatian tradition, such reflection is always for the purpose of *'action'*. We understand God as being active in the world, creating, loving and sustaining it, and ourselves as being called to be part of this action, of God's action, in the world. We understand that God is in all things, and all things are in God, i.e., the interconnectedness of all life.

If we engage in this approach, then from this foundation of a grounded and informed engagement with a changing world, a suffering world, a world throwing up new challenges, we can begin to imagine ourselves anew.

Moving from reimagining to renewing

From that point of a reimagined reality, the exercise of reviewing ourselves will throw a light on what needs to change, on where we have become stuck. It will illuminate a path forward, a path of renewal.

This renewal will become possible when we move to action ... not when we write a new vision or plan for ourselves, or a renewed mission statement, nor when we participate in formation training, but when we move into action.

So the idea of 'heart and head together for action' gives us the process for reimagining, reviewing and renewing our organisations. But as I said earlier, this process is intimately connected with the matter of our identity. Who are we anyhow? What is our purpose?

At first glance this fluid re-imagination process may sound at odds with how we might understand 'identity'. When we think of identity, what may spring to mind is something fixed or concrete: this is who we are, this is what we believe, this is what we do and we have the symbols and the rituals to prove it.

The research and literature on organisational identity can help us here. The concept of identity has been considered in many disciplines such as philosophy, cultural studies, psychology, sociology and anthropology. From the mid-1980s organisational identity as a field of study gained greater attention and with it the endeavour to answer the question: can an organisation, a company, have an identity? Or is it more that, when members claim an identity, this constitutes organisational identity?

Organisational identity

The roots of organisational identity research are largely to be found in the fields of sociology and social psychology with their emphasis on the social and contextual aspects of identity formation, though there have been broader influences in intervening decades.

A foundational article in the development of organisational identity theory, authored by Stuart Albert and David Whetten, was published in 1985.[50] The authors said that when people sought to identify the identity of an organisation, they looked for what is central, distinctive and enduring. They suggested that, when searching for an adequate statement of organisational identity, one is seeking to satisfy the following questions:

1. What is the essence of the organisation? The central character?

2. What distinguishes the organisation from others? What makes it distinctive?

3. What has remained the same over time? What is enduring?

---

[50] S. Albert and D.A. Whetten, 'Organizational Identity' in L.L. Cummings and B.M. Staw (eds), *Research in Organizational Behavior. An Annual Series of Analytical Essays and Critical Reviews*. Greenwich: JAI Press, 1985, 7, 263-295.

Identification of those elements that speak to what organisational identity is (i.e., what is central, distinctive, enduring about the organisation) can play into the notion of organisational identity being fixed. But the research and literature encourage an understanding that is more nuanced.

At one end of the spectrum there are those who, in attempting to define organisational identity, consider identity in terms of existential declarations (e.g. this is who/what we are). Others consider identity as a symbolic interpretation (e.g. this is what we mean/seem to mean to others). And others view organisational identity from the point of member reifications (e.g. we claim to be this or that).

From the field of organisational identity come many views. Here are a few:

- Organisational identity, far from being static and a given that we simply inherit, is something that is socially constructed, formed in relationship with others and in a constant state of 'becoming'.
- Organisational identity is formed through story telling; members tell stories about the organisation in their conversations, in what they write into their histories, records, formal documents and annual reports, and in what they put on their websites, in an effort to try to make sense of the organisational entity with which they are seeking to identify.
- An organisation has multiple narratives and multiple identities, not just one. For example, the various stakeholders might have different understandings of the organisation's identity: insiders (staff, volunteers, the Board), those who use the service, shareholders, the general public. And depending on, for example, the public profile of the organisation, there is increasing interest in pointing to the discrepancies between organisational image and organisational actions.
- Identity is something we do, not something we say we are, and it cannot be understood by reference to some reified statement or proclamation, but points to and is implemented

in the action of the group or organisation.

- More recently, alongside these approaches which look at a broad range of influences on organisational identity, we have seen a renewed interest in the idea of essence in understanding organisational identity, albeit with a more nuanced understanding of what has been referred to as the "complexity and dynamism" of organisational identity by Hatch and Schulz.[51]

I think I sit in this latter space, i.e. that when we talk about organisational identity we are talking about something essential to the organisation, and that this is grounded in our heritage and history, in relationships within the organisation and in relationship to our world. So organisational identity is both essential and dynamic.

But even when considering 'essence', what is central, distinctive and enduring, there is another dimension to this element. I would suggest that this essential part, rooted in our Ignatian heritage and history, is in itself dynamic, open, adaptive, responsive, not rigid, legalistic or constraining. This is because our heritage is not a set of rules; rather our heritage provides us with an orientation or an approach.

Returning to head and heart together for action

And this brings me back to where I started: 'heart and head together for action'. For those of us who walk in this Ignatian and Jesuit tradition, the central, distinctive and enduring elements are not a set of rules but an orientation. They encompass:

- being in relationship, being touched by the suffering of others;
- fostering attitudes of gratitude and the understanding of our interconnectedness;
- nurturing the longing in our hearts, and the hearts of others, for justice;

---

[51] M.J. Hatch and M. Schultz, 'The Dynamics of Organizational Identity', *Human Relations*, 2002, 55(8), 989-1018.

- being open to reading the signs of the times, doing the social analysis, the critical thinking;
- taking the time to reflect and discern what are our lived values, attitudes and behaviours;
- having the interior freedom and disposition to listen and learn, to change direction, to start over, to move to action, to speak truth to power.

This is our identity and while there may be different charisms among us and different approaches or emphases, much of this is shared across Catholic social service organisations.

So as we set about the task of reimagining ourselves in the face of a world where people continue to suffer and where our context is characterised by rapid change, growing disparity between rich and poor, and increasing marginalisation of particular persons and groups, let us dig deep into our roots to identify not necessarily what is in our strategic visions and plans, but what is central, distinctive and enduring about our organisations.

And let us make sure that we dig deep enough to get beyond platitudes or rules to an orientation that sees us reviewing ourselves (our lived values, attitudes and behaviours) in such a way that our path for action emerges: movement towards the poor, to relationship, to justice, to the nurturing and sustaining of our world, all the while understanding that with this action, and only with this action, comes our hope for renewing ourselves and our world.

Figure 1: Jesuit Social Services' Image of Deeply-rooted Identity

Mission in the Changing World:

Challenges to the Church

Confronting Family Violence: A Challenge for the Church to Make a Difference

*Helen Burt and Patrice Scales
with Bishop Vincent Long OFMConv*

If there was one community issue in Australia that demanded attention during 2015, it was that of family violence. With the announcement of the Victorian Royal Commission into Family Violence and Rosie Batty's award as 2015 Australian of the Year, family violence was at last given focus by the community and political parties. Family violence undermines the family unit as a safe sanctuary in which children can flourish, and family members feel loved, valued and safe. Family violence is therefore both a challenge and an opportunity for the Church to make a difference in an area in which it has a keen interest, but has not had a very active voice.

It was for these reasons that family violence was chosen as the topic for a public forum at Australian Catholic University on 24 February 2016 to launch the Catholic Social Services conference: *Review, Reimagine, Renew: Mission making a difference in a changing world.*

The forum was attended by more than 100 practitioners, parishioners, priests and members of religious orders, members of the University and the general public. It was chaired by Jocelyn Bignold, Chief Executive Officer of McAuley Community Services for Women, and addressed by a panel of skilled and experienced practitioners and advocates in the area of family violence. Panel members were invited to speak for 10 minutes about family violence from the point of view of their expertise in this area. The meeting was then opened to participants for questions and comments.

Those on the panel were:

Sr Michelle Reid, a Good Samaritan sister who is manager of the Good Samaritan Inn, a crisis accommodation house for homeless women and children, many of whom are escaping family violence

Paul Linossier, now Chief Executive Officer of Wesley Mission, who previously led the establishment of the Foundation for Prevention of Violence against Women and their Children (now known as Our Watch), and became the inaugural CEO of the Foundation in January 2014

Donella Johnston, Director of the National Office for the Participation of Women at the Australian Catholic Bishops Conference

Charlie King, sports commentator for the Australian Broadcasting Commission (ABC), and founder of the Northern Territory-born national campaign, 'No More to Family Violence'

Bishop Vincent Long OFMConv, at that time Episcopal Vicar for Social Services in the Archdiocese of Melbourne, who responded at the end of the forum on behalf of the Catholic Church.

Defining family violence

Family violence is not only violence perpetrated by men against women. Family violence can refer amongst other things to teenage violence against parents, women's violence against men, and elder abuse. However, prior to the forum, panel members agreed that the discussion would centre on the meaning of domestic and family violence as outlined in the National Plan to Reduce Violence against Women and their Children 2012-2022.[52]

The National Plan targets two main types of violence, domestic and family violence and sexual assault. The Plan says these are gender crimes in that they have an unequal impact on women. That being said, it is

---

[52] For details of the plan, see www.dss.gov.au/our-responsibilities/women/programs-services/reducing-violence/the-national-plan-to-reduce-violence-against-women-and-their-children-2010-2022; accessed on 10 May 2016.

important also to note that this reference point is not necessarily the starting point for Aboriginal communities.

There was an overriding acknowledgement by all panel members that our society is dealing with a most serious community issue that is taking the lives of too many women and has disastrous impacts on children. It was a stark reminder of the seriousness of the topic in which participants were to be engaged when Paul Linossier, as first speaker, opened his comments by saying:

> I hope the conversation this evening is an uncomfortable conversation. I hope this, because it can only be uncomfortable when what we are talking about is something that we can't relegate to just being another important social justice issue that we need to pay attention to. It will be an uncomfortable conversation if it goes far enough, because it drives to the heart of our culture, the heart of our social arrangements and our view of the human person; and it will be uncomfortable because the bias and dispositions that we are not in touch with are written so deep into our DNA that even when we think we are on board we can unintentionally perpetuate the very attitudes and views that foster the condition in the first place.
>
> So let's be clear, we're talking about men's violence against women, physical and sexual violence, and we're talking about a litany of controlling behaviours that exclude and denigrate and over time demoralise and abuse and marginalise women. This is a factor in many, if not most, cultures on our globe, and it is clearly present and strong in Australian culture.

The challenge of gender inequality

The theme of Paul Linossier's comments about gender inequality was referred to many times throughout the forum. As Paul said, "There is one overriding precondition that allows men's violence against women to be played out. This is the fact of gender inequality ... Unless we can deal with that bias and the inequity that results, we have no hope of turning off the tap".

The structural and cultural impediments that form the barrier to women's participation in society, in the home, in the workplace, were seen to be the starting point for tackling any change. Michelle Reid noted, "Gender inequality is the basis of this social epidemic [of violence towards women and children] and is impacted on by structural inequality, systems and institutional inequalities". But she also noted that we, as individuals, can play a huge part in changing this. "It begins with the individual; it begins with me and begins with you. How I am formed in my beliefs, my expectations and my understanding of how I should be treated as a woman, a child or a man. To stop violence against women and children, attitudes and behaviours of communities need to change. This is a huge task".

The structural barrier to women's participation in the Catholic Church with its male dominated leadership did not go unchallenged by the panel or the audience. Donella Johnston told the forum: "I think we have to acknowledge that the leadership in our Church is male in a structural sense, and I think we have to acknowledge that this does affect the culture of the organisation". She spoke about her own experience when she moved from Catholic education to her role as Director of the National Office for the Participation of Women. "I'd come from the feminised culture of Catholic education. I say 'feminised' because about 70 percent of staff in Catholic schools are women and many of our leaders are women in Catholic schools in Australia. And I came into an organisation where all the leaders were male. I answer to the 44 bishops of Australia, so that was quite a culture shock".

Donella also left those at the forum with a question to ponder about structure: "What are the structures that currently exclude women and girls from participating in decision-making, leadership and ministry in your parish, in your diocese, in your community?"

The gender inequality discussion was perhaps most explicitly summed up in the words of Paul: "There is a global occupational, private and public discrimination, based on gender. When we engage in the conversation and begin to unpack the issues we're talking about, it drives us to challenge ourselves, in our family and personal relationships and in our community and institutional relationships". Paul invited participants to watch a DVD produced by Our Watch called 'Let's change the story'.[53]

---

[53] 'Let's change the story: Violence against women in Australia' produced by Our Watch and available through the Our Watch website at www.ourwatch.org.au; accessed on 10 May 2016.

Prevention is possible

"Violence against women is serious and it is prevalent, and it is also preventable" – Sr Michelle Reid sgs

Despite the seemingly impenetrable barriers to bringing a halt to the incidence of family violence, there was a strong message that it can be prevented, albeit this is not an easy or short-term task. It was clear from the panel discussion that there must be a multi-layered approach to addressing the causes of family violence, to developing and implementing early intervention strategies, and to leadership across government, public policy development and the community at all levels.

With the political will to address family violence now being shown by politicians, a whole population approach is seen as being feasible. Paul Linossier believes the community can draw encouragement from other large-scale public health, whole population interventions that have a track record of success in Australia. "Whether it is the QUIT smoking campaign, drink driving, seatbelts or similar campaigns, there is evidence that multi-faceted, mutually reinforcing, whole population strategies can change both behaviours and attitudes, and there is a complex, non-linear relationship between those", he told the audience.

Hand in hand with whole population campaigns are the grass-root endeavours that aim to tackle the issue of prevention at a local level. The crisis accommodation service, the Good Samaritan Inn, took a decision to enter the area of prevention by initiating a schools-based respectful relationships project called the *We Can Do It* project. The initial three schools to be involved in the project were Catholic schools with a further three schools in the state school system, all in the northern suburbs of Melbourne, then commencing the program. Each of the schools that signed up agreed to contribute to the ongoing understanding of prevention in a whole school approach.

Rather than being a 'packaged' program, the project is tailored to each school community, to students and staff, and to the available resources of the particular schools. Local government and local health services are also involved and the Good Samaritan Inn plays the role of providing guidance and support. "Together we created the tools and safe environment that enabled the cultural shift to occur".[54]

"No more" – The Indigenous response to family violence

The Indigenous experience of using sport to send a message about family violence has grown into a positive program of social change throughout the Northern Territory. Charlie King is a proud Gurindji man. Before becoming an ABC sports commentator in 1994, Charlie was a child protection worker and worked in the area of family violence for many years. "When you do that sort of work, in child protection and family violence, it is not something that you just walk away from. It follows you like a shadow and is continuously asking you to do something [about it]", Charlie told the forum. Since 2008 he has combined the two areas of his work to tackle a difficult and pervasive problem in the Northern Territory.

In his career working in child protection and family violence services, Charlie noticed that when he attended public meetings in Darwin, Alice Springs and other parts of the Territory, 50 or 60 women would attend, and only two or three men. "It always bothered me why men didn't want to have a discussion about the issue of family violence, so that's what I wanted to ask men about as I travelled around the Northern Territory". So Charlie visited 38 communities in the Northern Territory over 12 months. It was when he sat down with the old men to explain the extent of the problem of family violence around Australia, that they would say to Charlie "no more, no more, no more". Charlie explained to the forum that 'no more' is the term that Aboriginal people use when they want to get rid of something, not just when they have had enough. When he visited other communities, Charlie would say, "You know those old fellows, when I talked about family violence, they say 'no more, no more', and the men would say, 'well, we need to link up, we all need to link up and do something about this'".

"This was another strong message for me, so we came up with the

---
[54] C. Dew, 2015. 'We Can Do It Respectful Relationships in Schools project: Evaluation report'. Melbourne: Good Samaritan Inn Ltd.

idea of asking sporting clubs to participate". Teams walked onto the ground and linked arms together at the elbow to make a strong symbolic statement that they, as men, say 'no more' to family violence. Police reported a drop in family violence incidents over the next two days. When two interstate teams, the Canberra Raiders and Parramatta Eels, played in Darwin, the teams linked arms saying 'no more' to family violence. And so the No More Campaign continued to be developed. But, as Charlie said of what was missing, "After two or three days things would go back to where they were before. We needed to come up with a plan that would stop things going back to where they were".

The next step was to develop an action framework, and borrowing (or as Charlie said, "stealing shamelessly") from Reconciliation Actions Plans, they developed Domestic Violence Action Plans. Sporting clubs wrote their own team plans which set down how they would reduce family violence in their own communities. One club wrote their action plan when one of its players spent three months in prison after being charged with family violence. When he returned to the club, the player spoke behind closed doors to all club players, including the women's team, to explain that what he had done had destroyed his life. This changed the thinking of the whole club from one where winning and being tougher and harder was the message, to a club that encourages families to be involved. Charlie acknowledges that the program of changing attitudes through sport will take time but says they are already seeing positive signs. "We ran ads in the lead up to Christmas Day in the Territory, set up with a coach talking to his players but he was actually talking to them about dealing with domestic violence, not winning the game. The police gave us a report that showed a significant reduction in family violence on Christmas Day compared to Christmas Day last year. So the little things we all do are really helpful".

In a later question to Charlie about the link between alcohol abuse and family violence asked by Fr Brian Lucas from Catholic Mission, Charlie responded that men in their communities are coming to the realisation that the excuse that "we were drinking and that's why it happened" is no longer acceptable. "They don't say that anymore because they know we just don't buy it anymore". But Charlie acknowledged that the difficulty for the Indigenous community is that alcohol is still available.

He concedes there is a lot more to be done, "but the positive thing that comes out of it is that men are starting to realise now there's no excuse hiding behind the alcohol and saying it is causing you to commit an act of domestic violence".

Engaging with men in the conversation

Bringing men into the conversation about family violence was seen by the forum to be an integral part of effecting change in community norms, expectations and behaviour. Yet doing this in an already patriarchal society where gender inequality is entrenched requires new ways of communicating and engaging with men. Panel members had interesting and insightful comments to make about the importance of the 'male voice' in speaking out and connecting with males.

In her presentation, Donella commented on the impact that the then Chief of the Army David Morrison had on her in the way he dealt with the scandals involving male cadets' and officers' violence against females. She found his message that "the standard you walk past is the standard you accept" as being a very powerful force in highlighting the need to change the culture of the defence force, and in speaking out about violence against women generally.

The Male Champions of Change (MCC) program, of which David Morrison is a part, seeks powerful voices in CEO and leadership roles to support gender equality by stepping alongside women to bring about this change. Between them, these current 'champions' employ 600,000 people and have significant influence in changing culture in the workplace. A guide produced by MCC called 'Playing our Part: Workplace Responses to Domestic and Family Violence' assists workplaces to play their part in reducing the prevalence and impact of domestic and family violence.[55]

It was also seen as critically important to support men who wanted to bring about change in male and female relationships and family violence. Charlie shared his experience of working with Indigenous communities

---

[55] Male Champions of Change. 'Playing our Part: Workplace Responses to Domestic and Family Violence', available via download from the Male Champions of Change website: www.malechampionsofchange.com; accessed on 10 May 2016.

where they have found that, out of perhaps 100 men, a group of five or six men feel very strongly there should be more done about making families safe, working with women, and stopping the violence. But he also found there were as many men who felt very strongly that nobody should do anything about it but let it just remain as it is. "Our work has been about empowering that first group and helping them get a louder voice in their community".

Paul noted that the style of men's engagement is critical:

> It needs to be in a mode of relationship that is partnership and collaboration and respect. There's some research ... which holds up time and time again, that young men particularly are more likely to listen to and take the message of a man speaking about these issues than a woman. Now, that is a product of the sorts of things we're talking about today but needs to be understood in communication strategies when we're engaging young people as a group, whether it is through social media or in a classroom or public situation.

Can the Church make a difference?

Panel members were in agreement that the Church can make a difference in combating family violence. At parish level, and despite the male-dominated leadership, Michelle saw potential for the clergy in Catholic parishes to do a great deal more to have gender equity, and to run their parish on a more collaborative, equal footing for all, male and female, youth and elderly.

Training of young clergy about the issue of gender equality and family violence was seen as a necessary education and formation step. Donella also saw the need for formation of people who work in parishes. "Sixty-one percent of the people in parishes are women, so male pastors are largely working with women in parishes. I think some ongoing education and formation are very important in giving our leaders the confidence that they are able to speak out about this important issue".

There was agreement about the need for the Catholic Church to be a strong public voice speaking out against family violence. In November

2014, the Australian Catholic Bishops Conference released a media statement in advance of the International Day for the Elimination of Violence against Women stressing that "violence against women has no place in our society".[56]

Charlie saw the voice of women in the Church as being crucially important. "I don't think you can sit back as women in the Church and allow what is happening here without making your voices heard, expressing your view on this ... I challenge you to do your bit in all of this". Charlie encouraged women, backed by men in the Church, to make their voices heard to the 44 Australian Bishops. "Change will come. It will come because it is right. So the time is here, the time is now, we can't leave it for another year".

Patrice Scales of Catholic Social Services Victoria noted that her organisation was working with the Bishops of Victoria on an initiative for the Church in Victoria, and that the forum itself was a step along that road.[57]

In concluding the panel session and with sincere thanks to the panel of presenters, Jocelyn introduced Bishop Vincent Long OFMConv, then Episcopal Vicar for Social Services in the Archdiocese of Melbourne, and invited him to address the forum on the Church's response to family violence. He did so in the following terms.

---

[56] Council for Australian Catholic Women, 2014. Media Statement: 'Elimination of Violence against Women', 20 November. Canberra: Australian Catholic Bishops Conference, Bishops Commission for Church Ministry, at www.catholic.org.au/acbc-media/downloads/all-downloads/bishops-1/media-releases-1/1584-elimination-of-violence-against-women-statement/file; accessed 1 July 2016.

[57] Since the forum developments have continued within the Catholic Church in Australia. The *Rewrite the Story* initiative by the Catholic Archdiocese of Brisbane [www.RewriteTheStory.org.au; accessed on 1 July 2016] joined initiatives such as Australian Catholic University's *Support for Victims of Family or Domestic Violence Policy* [www.acu.edu.au/policies/hr/leave/support_for_victims_of_family_or_domestic_violence; accessed on 1 July 2016].

How must the Church respond? – *Bishop Vincent Long OFMConv*

Domestic violence has often been considered a private issue and shrouded in silence. I was born and raised in Vietnam where family honour is paramount. I suspect this sense of family honour and reputation is common to many cultures. Even in places where it is not so strongly inculcated, we are often reluctant to air our family's 'dirty laundry' in public. The result is that many choose to stay silent in the face of family violence. Even when domestic violence is reported, sometimes there are failures to protect victims adequately or to bring perpetrators to justice swiftly.

When current statistics point towards one in six women having experienced domestic violence in Australia, we know there are both victims and perpetrators even within Church-based communities. How the Church and Christians respond to them is crucial in seeing justice, healing and transformation. In some cases, we have responded to domestic violence in wonderfully supportive ways for victims. However, sadly, there have been countless times when we have let women and children down, and sometimes put them even more at risk through disbelief, minimising the victim's experience, or staying silent.

This inadequate response must not continue. We believe that the first instinct of Christians must be a genuine compassion for those who have been harmed in our communities. We can support our communities to be equipped to be safe and affirming places for women to disclose abuse, where justice will be sought, action taken and real support offered. Victims need to have confidence that they will be heard and believed, that family violence will not be excused and victims will not be blamed.

Religion can be either a resource or a roadblock for battered women. As a resource, it can encourage women to resist mistreatment. As a roadblock, its misinterpretation can contribute to a victim's self-blame and suffering, and to the abuser's rationalisation. A correct reading of Scripture leads people to understand the equal dignity of men and women, and relationships based on mutuality and love. Biblical literalism and complementarianism, instead, provide the basis for systematic oppression or structural discrimination of women, leading communities, even church communities, to protecting perpetrators of domestic violence while simultaneously heaping shame and scorn upon its victims.

Jesus always protected the vulnerable and exposed evil. He always respected the human dignity of women. Consistently, he spoke and acted in favour of the vulnerable and challenged ingrained attitudes of prejudice and exclusion. We even see him breaking social taboos and expanding the boundaries of human love, acceptance and friendship.

Pope John Paul II reminds us: "Christ's way of acting, the Gospel of his words and deeds, is a consistent protest against whatever offends the dignity of women".[58] We want to follow the example of Jesus, our model for equal, loving and mutual human relationships. Clearly, Scripture and the example of Jesus challenge us to act in favour of the victims of injustice and violence. But they also caution us against any attempt that would prevent oppressed individuals from accessing higher levels of inclusion and human flourishing.

The root causes of violence against women have often been found to be gender inequity and rigid gender stereotypes. Furthermore, violent attitudes and behaviours have their root in the same place, the abuse of power and control of one person over another.

How can the Church be the model of inclusion, empowerment and human flourishing, especially for those who are oppressed? Can Church leaders, who are mostly male, be champions of change on the issue of family violence and its root causes of gender inequity and rigid gender stereotypes?

The example of Jesus in relating to women and caring for the most vulnerable, even at the cost of defying cultural expectations, provides us with the guiding principle in our work of rooting out injustice and violence. Religious leaders have a sacred duty to protect the vulnerable and emulate Jesus' humble, inclusive and boundary-breaking leadership.

It pertains to us as believers to implement the full vision of God's kingdom. St Paul summarises the kingdom vision of Jesus in *Galatians*

---

[58] Pope John Paul II, 1988. Apostolic Letter: *Mulieris Dignitatem*, Section 15. Vatican City: Vatican; accessed on 10 May 2016 at w2.vatican.va.

3:28: "There is neither Jew nor Greek, slave nor free, male nor female, for you are all one in Christ Jesus". Jesus' death brought with it equality for Jews and Gentiles, but it was only with time, and extreme struggle and sacrifice on the Church's part, that this whole vision began to become a reality.

Our work for the full realisation of the kingdom in all its aspects remains to be accomplished. The vision and example of Jesus inspires us as we confront both the manifestations and the root causes of injustice and violence and make a difference to the society in which we live.

Addressing and Preventing Sexual Abuse

Gabrielle McMullen

with Robert Fitzgerald and Maria Harries

Setting the scene

In February 2016 Australia's Royal Commission into Institutional Responses to Child Sexual Abuse had been in operation for over three years. It had received over 29,000 phone calls and some 16,000 letters; it had held close to 5,000 private sessions and referred nearly one thousand matters to authorities including police. Further, the Royal Commission had considered 36 major case studies, each associated with a least one public hearing; one third of the case studies considered instances of sexual abuse in the Catholic Church.[59]

This focus on the Catholic Church reflects, in part, the extensive reach during the second half of the twentieth century of the schools, orphanages, social services and parishes of the Church. Significantly, however, this concentration on the Catholic Church particularly relates to findings by the Royal Commission and previous State-based investigations that the Church has a record of child sexual abuse disproportionally higher than for other comparable institutions and, in numerous instances, that its responses to the abuse had been grossly inappropriate. For the Churches generally, the scandal of the child sexual abuse has the further aspect of their failure to live out the Christianity which is the heart of their very existence.

In the week commencing 22 February 2016 the Royal Commission was conducting its third face-to-face session in Ballarat related to Case Study 28 considering "the response of the Catholic Diocese of Ballarat

---

[59] For further details in relation to the Royal Commission into Institutional Responses to Child Sexual Abuse, see www.childabuseroyalcommission.gov.au; accessed on 27 March 2016.

and other Catholic Church authorities in Ballarat to allegations of child sexual abuse against clergy or religious".[60] Ballarat in central Victoria was well represented at the conference held during that week in Melbourne[61] that included a forum on sexual abuse, on which this Chapter is based.

The Ballarat-related hearing continued in the following week with Cardinal George Pell giving evidence by video link from Rome concerning Case Study 28: Catholic Church Authorities in Ballarat as well as Case Study 35: Catholic Archdiocese of Melbourne.[62] Originally a priest of the Diocese of Ballarat, Cardinal Pell had subsequently been Archbishop of both Melbourne and Sydney, prior to his appointment to the Vatican as Prefect of the Secretariat for the Economy. In 1996, as Archbishop of Melbourne, he had introduced the Melbourne Response, an Archdiocesan process for assisting people sexually abused by its priests or staff.[63] Along with other Church leaders, Cardinal Pell was interrogated by the Royal Commission on his knowledge of historical sexual abuse of minors in each of the dioceses and on the Church's response.

The same week saw the film *Spotlight* receiving Academy Awards for Best Picture along with Best Original Screenplay. This film recounts the Pulitzer Prize-winning, year-long *Boston Globe* investigation into sexual abuse in the local Catholic Church which in 2002 rocked the city of Boston and had implications for the Church worldwide. The investigation exposed decades-long covering-up, with not only the Church but also the police, media, legal profession and politicians implicated. In his review of the film, Peter Sheehan, an Associate of the Australian Catholic Office for Film and Broadcasting, concluded:

---

[60] Royal Commission, 2016. 'Case Study 28 (Catholic Church authorities in Ballarat)', at www.childabuseroyalcommission.gov.au; accessed on 27 March 2016.
[61] The Catholic Social Services conference, *Review, Re-imagine, Renew: Mission making a difference in a changing world*, which inspired this volume, was held in Melbourne on 24-26 February 2016.
[62] Royal Commission, 2016. 'Case Study 35 (Catholic Archdiocese of Melbourne)', at www.childabuseroyalcommission.gov.au; accessed on 27 March 2016.
[63] For information on the Melbourne Response, see www.cam.org.au/Professional-Standards/Melbourne-Response; accessed on 29 March 2016.

This is a film that pushes one to think long and hard, and critically about the behaviour of the Catholic Church. It shows the danger of Faith, when it is practiced blindly, and it makes the points dramatically and tellingly that: all abuse should stop; the Catholic Church should recognise everything that has happened; and the Church never should behave in such a way again.[64]

Like the Royal Commission, the film has highlighted the tragic life-long impact of sexual abuse on victims and their families and the failure of institutions like the Catholic Church to recognise and respond appropriately to "truly a horrible crime" (Pope Francis).[65]

Responding to the sexual abuse crisis

The ministry of Catholic Social Service agencies contributes to the Church's response to the sexual abuse crisis at the coalface on a daily basis. In planning the 2016 Catholic Social Services conference, *Review, Re-imagine, Renew: Mission making a difference in a changing world*, it was self-evident that 'Addressing and Preventing Sexual Abuse' would be a significant part of the program.

As indicated above, the Royal Commission is a national Government response to addressing and preventing sexual abuse in institutions. At the time of its creation one response of the Australian Catholic Church was to establish the Truth Justice and Healing Council, which is coordinating the Church's response to the Royal Commission "with a commitment to justice and compassion for survivors".[66] Established jointly by the Australian Catholic Bishops Conference and Catholic Religious Australia (the peak body for leaders of religious congregations in Australia), the 11-member Council includes "men and women with professional and other expertise in the areas of child sexual abuse, paedophilia, trauma, mental

---

[64] P.W. Sheehan, 2016. '2016 Film Reviews: *Spotlight*'. North Sydney: Australian Catholic Office for Film and Broadcasting; accessed on 29 March 2016 at www.catholic.org.au/film-reviews-2016/spotlight-peter-sheehan.

[65] Pope Francis, 2014. 'Interview of Pope Francis with journalists during the return flight from the Holy Land', 26 May. Vatican City: Vatican; accessed on 29 March 2016 at w2.vatican.va.

[66] For information on the Truth Justice and Healing Council, see www.tjhcouncil.org.au; accessed on 29 March 2016.

illness, suicide, education, public administration and governance".[67]

As at the Catholic Social Services conference, this chapter brings together some insights into sexual abuse and the response of the Catholic Church arising from two key perspectives, namely:

- Royal Commissioner Robert Fitzgerald, who brings a background in commerce, law, public policy and community services to his role, and

- member of the Truth Justice and Healing Council Dr Maria Harries, a senior social worker with particular expertise in child and family wellbeing and mental health and currently also chair of Catholic Social Services Australia.

The following represents an edited version of some of the key issues and perspectives addressed at the conference by each of these two speakers.

A perspective from a Royal Commissioner – *Robert Fitzgerald*

I wish to give a brief reflection on the work of the Commission but stress that the Commission is some way from finalising its findings and recommendations. These will be provided to the Government and thereafter published in full at the end of the Commission's life late next year.

The Royal Commission into Institutional Responses to Child Sexual Abuse has already conducted 4,800 private interview sessions, held over 30 public hearings/case studies and commissioned 100 pieces of research. Some 13,000 allegations of abuse had been received in relation to 3,900 institutions. Approximately 40 percent deal with abuse in out-of-home care settings such as foster care, orphanages and children's homes. Further, 900 matters had been referred to the police in various jurisdictions.

In relation to Catholic institutions, as a Commissioner who is a practicing Catholic with previous voluntary involvement in faith-based community services, I have, to date, exempted myself from taking a role

---

[67] Ibid.

in cases studies (public hearings) which have had a primary focus on the Catholic Church, except for St Ann's Special School in Adelaide, as I possess useful knowledge in this disability field.

The work of the six Commissioners concludes in mid-December 2017 and each one of us will be working untiringly until that end date. Some of our findings and recommendations have and will be released progressively. To date we have published final reports on working with children's checks, redress and civil litigation reforms, with more to come, and many research reports also.

Of course, the significant problem of child sexual abuse is not exclusive to the Catholic Church, indeed the evidence of widespread abuse in all forms of institutions has been made clear from the Commission's work to date. Yet anyone who has even a cursory interest in these issues would know that the Catholic Church is at the centre of much of public discussion. So far 60 percent of private session allegations relate to non-government agencies, the largest grouping by far being against Catholic Church institutions. Not only do the numbers show why the Church is front and centre in these considerations but the Church's initial responses have been found to be wanting and often exacerbated the pain and suffering of victims. Further, abuse within faith-based institutions represents a genuine betrayal of trust not only to those directly impacted by the abuse but also to the wider community.

Whilst more recent responses have shown that the Catholic Church, along with other religions and institutions, is learning from the lessons of the past and responses are significantly more victim-focussed generally, much more remains to be done to bring justice for those abused and to create safe environments for children in the future.

Each institution needs to take responsibility for making reparation for past wrongs through understanding more fully what has really happened, providing appropriate redress and putting in place the necessary cultural and procedural reforms to reduce the likelihood of such crimes taking place in the future. We see a role for all governments to provide redress and support, together with individual agencies, and collectively to work for a better response to child sexual abuse including preventing further abuse in the future.

Understanding the past

Today it is too early to draw firm conclusions about the past. That is the very work we are undertaking. And we have many more private sessions and public hearings ahead of us. Yet I have been asked to make some observations that may be relevant to Catholic social services and I draw largely from my own experience in the hundreds of private sessions that I have been privileged to be part of to date. The following are just some brief headline points:

- The rights of children were limited and not sufficiently valued to protect them against more powerful individuals who had the support and protection of trusted institutions. In some circumstances children were told that they were no good, nobody wanted them or nobody cared what happened to them.

- Whilst many children who were abused were simply in the wrong place at the wrong time, many had vulnerabilities that offenders exploited, especially in residential care settings. Many came from impoverished families, domestic violence, recent family separations or other already traumatic environments. They were targeted and exploited. For some their early sexual abuse made them more vulnerable to further abuse in other settings and over time.

- Some children were seeking love and affection and fell easy prey to offenders who either manipulated such desires or failed to maintain boundaries that should have been clear and unbreakable.

- Many children who were abused did not feel they could tell anyone and many who did were not believed and some punished for daring to say such terrible things. This often applied when parents, teachers or carers were informed. Even police sometimes sent them back to their abusers without question. Almost none knew how to disclose safely.

- Offenders were sometimes very charismatic, especially some coaches, teachers, priests and ministers, and often well-liked;

and groomed families, children and their colleagues. Building family trust allowed extraordinary access to children.

- In older cases especially, brutal and humiliating punishments were part of the culture of the institutions and some offenders used their power, force and violence to both offend and demand silence.

- Some cases involved grooming, touching and fondling of many victims, often in class rooms and semi-public places, without the perpetrator ever being reprimanded. Grooming was not well-understood and even today many are not well-trained in this area.

- Older teenagers, both boys and girls, who were abused post-puberty were often treated as the culprit or accused of making advances, rather than as victims of those in trusted positions whose duty it was to maintain boundaries. Some abuse lasted over years even going into late teenage-hood, showing the complexity of such abusive relationships.

- Abuse by older children of younger children is a not uncommon theme for those in out-of-home care settings and some boarding schools. Bullying is often experienced by children abused and, if bullying is not dealt with, children do not believe that the institution will do anything about abuse.

- Institutions either failed to act or, if they did, they resolved the offending by removing the offender from the premises or transferring them to another place of work but rarely reporting them. Sometimes references were even given to new employers.

- Some in authority and some offenders believed that sexual abuse was only a moral failing but not a crime. Some people seemed not to believe that anything short of sexual penetration was sex. (The influence of the then Church's teachings on human sexuality and the formation of clergy and religious regarding sexuality generally will be the subject of further review.) Some people in authority and others also believed that sexualised initiation ceremonies and hazing were not abuse and people should just get over it.

- Many institutional leaders believed sexual abuse should be dealt with in-house and that reporting such matters would harm their reputations or that of their institutions. Even more so, some believed victims were exaggerating their claims and, even when many came forward, preferred the good standing of the accused over the evidence of the victims. Old boys and old girls in some schools may also have held such views.

- Children in out-of-home care were often at greater risk and feared reporting matters either because they would be punished or the placement would break down, with no certainty the next one would be any better. Often case workers failed to interview children by themselves, rather only conducting interviews in the presence of carers, who may have been one of the abusers.

- Most people who are abused take decades to report their abuse and most who have come to private Royal Commission sessions have neither reported the matters to the police nor put in claims against institutions, at least this stage. Wrongly, the failure to report in a timely way was seen as evidence of a lack of credibility of the victim.

The impacts of child sexual abuse can be long lasting and profound and the trauma associated with abuse can have severe mental health effects, impair the ability to have healthy relationships, and affect education and work prospects. Sometimes suicide has been a tragic consequence. Traumatic memories can come back like a roaring train later in life and the impacts can be considerable on these individuals, and those they love. If there is good news, many, despite the enormity of the traumatic impacts, have achieved much and the capacity to keep on going is inspiring.

For some, however, the impacts are less severe. Indeed, there are many who have lived very productive lives and managed the impacts very well and their resilience needs to be acknowledged. There is no one response and no one event type accurately predicts those impacts.

Nevertheless, ongoing good supports are a critical factor in determining a person's ability to deal with the impacts over a lifetime.

Lessons learned so far

It is understood from these cases and the many matters brought to the Commission that there are a multiplicity of motivations and methods of operation utilised by those who have sexually abused children, and this will be the focus of further study by the Commission. Trying to understand offenders and offending is complex yet important if we are to make real progress in reducing the risk to children. Many of those who abused in Catholic institutions were effective in covering up their behaviour and may have actively groomed their colleagues, as they did families and children, creating high levels of trust.

Many priests, brothers and sisters have been astonished that their colleagues abused children. The abusive members of their communities were able to fool those around them seemingly with ease.

However, this was made easier where many lacked the skills to identify suspect behaviours, failed to question and call into line those acting inappropriately, failed to listen to or believe children, and ultimately failed to recognise the acts as crimes rather than mere moral failings. There were few preventative practices put in place and warning signs, whereby the offender's actions were not consistent with the Church's values, were often overlooked.

Brutal and humiliating punishments in many children's homes and some schools fostered an environment where children were not respected and abusive conduct too often overlooked. Even though community standards were different during the period when many of these crimes took place, the high level of violence in these institutions was entirely unacceptable even then. Further, it did not occur at many other schools or institutions at the time. Why were some facilities caring, nurturing and respectful of children whilst others were brutal and demeaning within the same timeframe and same faith?

Too often the offenders were members of institutions where culture, practices and procedures were tragically insufficient or inadequate. In some cases complaints and evidence of misbehaviour were presented, and observable, over many years but to no avail. People were also frightened to blow the whistle on their colleagues. And poor governance arrangements and a lack of a transparent culture contributed. An institution that values secrecy over openness will always be a dangerous place for vulnerable people and enable bad practices.

Many leaders of institutions have claimed that they knew nothing of the abuse going on under their watch. Yet some of these leaders failed to establish a culture and processes that ensured allegations of abuse were brought to the top. People working in such institutions understood that they should not take up issues that may result in adverse publicity, whilst some were discouraged from rocking the boat for fear of reprisals against themselves. The notion of 'plausible deniability' may also have been present in some institutional leadership approaches.

Preventing abuse in the future

The Commission will be examining many aspects of the Church and other institutions to understand better why abuse occurred and will make findings and recommendations accordingly. However, I just wish to raise some points already apparent from our work in relation to prevention.

Any institution, when challenged, will state that they are working in the best interests of the client group they are serving. However, the reality is, from the accounts heard by the Commission, that some institutions have put other priorities, including reputation, ahead of the best interests of children whose care and wellbeing should have been paramount. There are also instances where there are or were very real conflicts of interest embedded in the governance arrangements, including of some churches, which have prevented correct action being taken.

Prevention starts by ensuring the interests and rights of children are indeed paramount in the governance, culture and practices of the institution. From boardroom to every interface with a child, this commitment to acting in their best interest is critical to creating a child-safe environment.

And further, where abuse has occurred either historically or more recently, the institution must act to support the person affected and act in their interests to minimise further adverse impacts and to seek just remedies. Caring for the complainant, proper investigation, proper reporting and so on are essential. Governance bodies must understand their duties not only legally but also those required by the values and mission of the Church. They must seek the best legal and other advice but must receive that advice and act upon it in a manner consistent with their stated mission and values. Legal advice must always be understood in the context in which it is to be applied.

Minimum standards and best practices need to be documented, implemented and monitored across all aspects of the Church and institutional life engaged with children. The Victorian Government has recently legislated in this area and some other States, Queensland and South Australia, have some minimum child-safe standards in place. More needs to be done and the Commission will be presenting research and recommendations in relation to creating a child-safe environment in all institutions that deal regularly with children. Australian Children's Commissioners have already done much work. Elements of such a child-safe framework may include the following areas:

- organisational leadership, governance and culture,
- children's participation and empowerment,
- human resources management,
- child-safe policy and procedures,
- education and training,
- family and community involvement,
- physical and online environment,
- review and continuous improvement,
- child-focused complaint process.

These are in addition to the requirements for proper working-with-children and police checks already required by law. Obviously already schools, foster care agencies and child care centres must comply with many such requirements but a child-safe environment is necessary in all areas of Church activities, modified and adapted according to the different settings and contexts. What will be important is that members of the Church community, users of Church services and the broader community should have ready access to such policies. Easy-to-understand guidance will be essential as in the anti-bullying campaigns.

The Commission readily acknowledges improvements that have been made by governments and institutions in recent years and even since the Commission commenced. We acknowledge work being undertaken, as we meet, by the Catholic Church in creating safer environments for children in their services.

Finally, what of the need for restoration and healing? Many victims of abuse experience a lack of peace in their lives. Apart from redress, including ongoing access to support and counselling, not all but some of these victims and survivors of abuse, especially older people, seek reconnection of some kind with the Church of their childhood. Many seek a return to faith rather than engagement with the formal church. But others seek more. Catholic organisations need to engage sensitively and constructively with this real need for healing where sought by victims and survivors and be open to their needs and requests.

A perspective from a Truth Justice and Healing Council member

– *Dr Maria Harries*

In the main those engaged in Catholic social services in Australia have a passion for working at what Pope Francis calls 'the periphery'. We work with individuals and families who are wounded and struggling, generally materially impoverished and marginalised, and often, and quite understandably, spiritually bereft as well. Importantly, many of those we serve are victims of trauma, family violence, sexual assault and other forms of abuse. In escaping hostile environments, many are separated from family, homeless and profoundly vulnerable. Our myriad services providing material and counselling assistance to these individuals and families are staffed by young and not-so-young women and men of Catholic or other faiths or who ascribe to no faith. Regardless of our different faith journeys, our very visceral endeavours are grounded in the call of Catholic Social Teaching that challenges the moral indifference to poverty, violence and disadvantage in much of our society. At the core of this mission is deeply relational service imbued with the essential spirit of love and compassion of which Pope Francis talks.

Challenging questions

How then do we, and our colleagues, make sense of the litany of sexual abuses perpetrated by members of our Catholic community that have been reported to the Royal Commission into Institutional Responses to Child Sexual Abuse? We all know that the abuse of children and the trafficking of children and young women and men are endemic in contemporary society. And many of us have worked hard to help heal people from the impact of these horrors and to advocate for services for victims as well as preventative measures. But now we must deal with hearing that these abuses have been committed on a large scale by leaders and others within our cherished Church, particularly by members of the clergy. Countless unspeakable acts of sexual violence have been perpetrated on children and young people. That many adults who were the victims of child abuse are now able to tell their story is largely due to self-advocacy initiatives and the work of the Royal Commission. How do we make sense of their experiences, understand the historical denial of abuse, and deal with the seeming protection that has been provided to perpetrators in the name of saving our Church from 'scandal'?

I ask these questions, in the first instance, not because I place them as the most important ones for our services, but because, whilst often unspoken, the broader questions about 'how' and 'why' are on the lips of so many of us. It all seems barely possible to believe. How do we reconcile the emerging reality of systemic abuse within our Church, accommodate it within our faith journey, and embrace it within the charter of our Catholic social services? There can be no doubt that this desperately serious issue needs to be talked about as we work out ways to address the needs of those who have directly experienced the abuse and the countless others on whom the abuse impacts: victims' children, spouses, parents, extended families, communities and parishes. And it has to be addressed if we are to help victims towards healing as well as prevent abuse occurring in the future.

Facing the reality

Sharing these questions with a colleague who had experienced such abuse, his answer was simple and yet profound. His proposition was, "First you need to accept the evidence and the reality". How very sensible and yet how hard this is for many of us. The theory of cognitive dissonance helps us understand the very uncomfortable tension that comes from holding two conflicting thoughts at the same time. How can we manage the tension emerging from the conflicting thought that such appalling acts have been perpetrated by those who held positions of leadership and authority in our Church? Some of us refuse to believe, many of us have retreated from our faith and yet others of us appear to be able to sit with the discomfort and find other ways of understanding and helping in the healing.

Once we can face these facts, of primary importance is the recognition of the harm that has been done and the need for listening to, believing and healing the terrible wounds of victims who are survivors. As we confront the appalling reality of sexual abuse in our Church community, and apologise for the failings of our own systems of care, all of us in Catholic social services are called on to recognise the pain and suffering caused to so many. As well we must manage our own distress and that of uncomprehending colleagues as we embrace the responsibility of continuing the vital healing work that we must undertake. We must not capitulate to the view that, because these terrible acts have been perpetrated within our Church, we cannot be engaged in healing. Survivors will make their own choices about what services to access and many are asking for assistance that recognises the violation that occurred within a Church to which they may well continue to belong. There are already some great initiatives amongst our services. A hallmark for those at the forefront of these initiatives is that they engaged early with learning from the experiences of survivors themselves.

New supervising entity

Commissioner Robert Fitzgerald has provided us with an unambiguous summary of the publicly available abuse data relevant to us all. And he has highlighted the importance of prevention if we are to avoid this terrible blight recurring. Placing a priority on prevention, the Australian Catholic Bishops Conference and Catholic Religious Australia have accepted a recommendation from the Truth, Justice and Healing Council to create a new supervising entity for professional standards for the Australian Catholic Church. As an independent national agency set up as a company limited by guarantee, it will establish and monitor standards for all services delivered to children and vulnerable people under the auspices of the Catholic Church. The agency will impact on all of us and it is important we understand that it is an essential development as we aim to prevent all forms of abuse and re-establish our credibility and trustworthiness. Importantly, it will not duplicate the already significant compliance requirements of various government regulations but instead will utilise established standards, ensure there is national consistency, and augment them with the Gospel values that are fundamental to our Church ministries.

During this Royal Commission, the governance structures of the Catholic Church have been sorely challenged, as well they should be, given the extent of our failures. The new supervising entity is one element of a strategy for safeguarding children and vulnerable people. As its details are fleshed out in the coming months, our governance structures will be further tested. We need to be prepared to help lead the Church into a governance structure that ensures a safe and nourishing place for children and vulnerable adults and for all of us. As leaders in Catholic social services it is vital for us to acknowledge the strength and knowledge of our people and our lay leadership, to fight vigorously and courageously to promote sustainable, inclusive cultures, and to eschew the gendered and other power imbalances that provide such fertile grounds for abuse. In the light of the already dire findings of the Royal Commission, our call to mission and to making a difference has taken on new meaning and urgency and I know we can and must help lead the Church into a safer and healing future.

Conclusion

Australian society and the Catholic Church are fortunate to have those like Robert Fitzgerald and Maria Harries and their colleagues on the Royal Commission and Truth Justice and Healing Council, respectively, whose efforts are helping to redress past failures and ensure protection of children and vulnerable people into the future.

The Church in Australia faces a large agenda. This must include full recognition of the errors and evils that have transpired, and a compassionate and professional approach to victims and survivors. Catholic social service agencies have much to offer in relation to the latter – they must be assertive in taking an appropriate part in the response of the broader Church.

In moving forward the Catholic Church is also seeking to put in place best practice with respect to its ministries to children and vulnerable people. One key development, as mentioned above by Maria Harries, is the proposed establishment of a supervising entity, independent of Church institutions, to care for, protect and support children and vulnerable people to whom the Church ministers. Again, Catholic social service agencies are called to be an effective part of this response.

International developments as well are critical to changing the culture of the Church and in 2014 Pope Francis established the Pontifical Commission for the Protection of Minors,[68] which is led by Cardinal Sean O'Malley OFMCap, who was appointed to Boston to address the crisis there that was featured in *Spotlight*.

Dialogue with victims of sexual abuse is critical to both healing and

---

[68] For information on the Pontifical Commission for the Protection of Minors, see w2.vatican.va/content/francesco/en/letters/2014/documents/papa-francesco_20140322_chirografo-pontificia-commissione-tutela-minori.html#Statutes; accessed on 29 March 2016.

transforming the Church and Pope Francis and his predecessor Pope Benedict XVI have met with victims. At a Mass for victims in Rome on 7 July 2014, Pope Francis stated:

> Your presence here speaks of the miracle of hope, which prevails against the deepest darkness. Surely it is a sign of God's mercy that today we have this opportunity to encounter one another, to adore God, to look in one another's eyes and seek the grace of reconciliation.
>
> Before God and his people I express my sorrow for the sins and grave crimes of clerical sexual abuse committed against you. And I humbly ask forgiveness.
>
> I beg your forgiveness, too, for the sins of omission on the part of Church leaders who did not respond adequately to reports of abuse made by family members, as well as by abuse victims themselves. This led to even greater suffering on the part of those who were abused and it endangered other minors who were at risk.[69]

As we move into the future and seek to address past sexual abuse and promote a culture of no tolerance, may we be inspired by survivors of sexual abuse whose courageous actions are leading to a transformation of the Church and society.

---

[69] Pope Francis, 2014. 'Homily of Pope Francis', Domus Sanctae Marthae, Rome, 7 July. Vatican City, Vatican; accessed on 29 March 2016 at w2.vatican.va.

The Mission or the Money or Both

Tony Nicholson

A telling parable

In the early 1980s, a series of Ecumenical Lenten Studies held in the inner city developed into a discussion about the issues facing these local communities. People became quite animated. They were able to see the needs and they wanted to move from talk to action. They were convinced that, together, as members of these inner city communities, they really could make a difference if they pooled their various talents and skills and worked cooperatively.

After a short time, the group decided to tackle youth homelessness in the area. All types of people became involved, not just the church-goers. Each found a role with everyone accommodating the gifts and talents of each other. Funds were raised, a sprawling old house was rented and, within months of the first discussion, a group of about thirty volunteers found themselves running a youth refuge that accommodated half a dozen young people each night. After a short period of time, one paid employee was recruited but time, money and goods continued to be given by the community in abundance.

These were heady and sometimes chaotic days for both the teenagers and the volunteers. Mistakes were undoubtedly made but there was evident goodwill aplenty, along with lots of laughs and some tears.

Yet, in all of this, something important was unfolding. The authenticity of it all spoke to those young people, this demonstration that ordinary people in the community really valued them. And, more than this, they valued them enough to act unselfishly on their behalf. And, of course, the ordinary community values and expectations that these people brought to their volunteering meant that sometimes there were misunderstandings and conflict, and some activities were misplaced. But in spite of this or, more likely, because of it, the young people responded to the authenticity of it all, to the genuine concern of these volunteers. It was new to them, but they instinctively grasped what was happening around them and for them.

In that first year or two, young lives were turned around. New connections were made to the community and some got jobs with local employers. Some resumed their education at local schools and volunteers tutored them. Some joined local sports clubs and one or two got themselves into trouble with the local police. But, for the first time for most of them, there was always a local person, one of the volunteers, available to try to put a benevolent spin on their alleged wrongdoing.

Over thirty years on, and most of those involved in the youth refuge, both volunteers and the young people, now in their middle-age, look back fondly on those days.

However, the story does not end there. Within eighteen months of beginning the endeavour, matters to do with finances, insurances and other governance issues, came to the fore. The volunteers realised that they needed an established organisation both to assist them and to take the project to the next level. Volunteer labour alone was not sufficient to maintain and develop the service. And so the youth refuge was taken under the wing of a well-established community service organisation which provided the governance and administrative support required, as well as bringing to the endeavour more resources and skills.

Before long, however, things began to change. Government funding became available, several professional staff were employed, a case management approach was adopted and the role of volunteers was regulated and narrowly prescribed. While the service's capacity was built, the ethos of the enterprise changed. It had been professionalised. The message to the volunteers was clear and dismaying. What they had brought to the lives of these young people, their willingness to help in any way they could, investing in making a difference in their lives through their voluntary care, was no longer needed, required or particularly valued.

Inevitably, they drifted away and the refuge service very quickly evolved into a now familiar welfare model of paid professionals, case managing their young, homeless clients, under rules specified by a government funding agency. The service's roots in the local community were largely severed and from then on, it operated in isolation.

A flawed paradigm

Is this but a nostalgic tale, romanticising times past? Or is it rather a parable of where we find the community services sector today? Surely the latter, for indeed, models of care, funding, governance and the relationship between the community itself and community service agencies are all critical factors in this tale.

The community services sector has evolved to what is now a critical stage, underpinned by a particular paradigm. Central to this paradigm is the idea that the sector can continue to meet society's present and emerging needs by contracting to government, expanding and aggregating organisations, driving for greater efficiency and further professionalising, regulating and circumscribing the care it provides. This is a paradigm that is fundamentally flawed. Whilst it may have served the sector well over the previous thirty years, especially by driving improvement in the quality, scope and reach of services, it cannot support the sector into the next thirty years. Why is this?

There are a number of important reasons why this model cannot take us into the future but the three key reasons are these: firstly, the paradigm is not sustainable; secondly, its loss of authentic connectedness to local community means that it is not a desirable model to take the sector forward; and thirdly, it does not have the capacity to deliver on the promise to meet the present and emerging needs of society.

The paradigm is not sustainable

The current paradigm, which depends upon employing paid professionals to work with the most vulnerable members of our communities, depends upon the availability of a workforce and, interrelated to this, corresponding levels of funding to employ them.

Firstly, we turn to the question of an available workforce. As the population ages, and the proportion of people of workforce age declines, the uncomfortable question arises as to where these workers are going to be found. Although this question will be faced by many sectors, businesses and industries, as an aging population affects them all, it has a particular resonance for the community services sector as competition for labour heats up. In such circumstances, the community services sector will never be able to match the remuneration offered by for-profit organisations and government departments. The risk is that professionals in the sector will vote with their feet resulting in the sector experiencing high staff turnover, skills shortages and even an outright shortage of available labour. This will inevitably lead to a diminution of standards. In some social services, especially those addressing very complex and demanding needs, these pressures are already being experienced. Over time, the services are likely to diminish. They will simply not be able to attract and afford the kind of professional staff they need to operate their models of care.

Secondly, there is the funding question. We must ask ourselves if governments will be prepared, or even have the capacity, to meet the cost of the expansion of the current models of service provision to meet the needs of an ever-expanding population. The rate of expansion of the population in Victoria alone is predicted to be around two percent per year. Speaking at a Brotherhood of St Laurence seminar, Professor John Daley from the Grattan Institute succinctly laid out the fiscal challenge facing Australian Governments over the next ten years. They will need to find four percent of GDP in savings and tax increases to balance their books by 2023.[70] States and Territories, as the major funding sources for community services, will be the hardest hit. We already have numerous examples of stretched State budgets failing, or unable, to make adequate provision for the real cost of the community services that they contract out to the sector.

The writing is surely on the wall. Funding the current practitioner-intensive service models to meet the needs of a growing population will be seen as prohibitively expensive and, ultimately, unsustainable.

For these two reasons alone, the lack of skilled employees and the cost of such practitioner-intensive models of service delivery, the community services paradigm presently in place will become unviable.

---

[70] J. Daley, 2013. *Australian Welfare Spending Trends: Past Changes, Future Drivers*, Brotherhood of St Laurence Seminar, 8 August; accessed on 5 September 2016 at grattan.edu.au/wp-content/uploads/2014/05/524_presentation_daley_BSL_130808.pdf.

Not a desirable model

It is indisputable that the community services sector has made positive gains through the professionalisation of care but it has just as clearly lost much. The youth refuge parable illustrates how easily the valuable contribution of volunteers and connection to local community can be lost by surrendering services to the community services sector. Apart from the diverse networks and local connections that a broad community involvement can contribute, there is also that intangible quality of authenticity experienced by the young people in the refuge parable that is a result of the caring relationships developed by volunteers. Something of the richness and spontaneity of such relationships is lost through professionalisation of care.

Many of the recognisable community service agencies, with which we are very familiar, were originally established by committed and caring members of local communities. They recognised a need and gathered ordinary people to meet it. The Brotherhood of St Laurence, founded by Fr Gerard Tucker, is a great example of this.[71] It was originally established to strengthen the ability of local parishes to respond to the needs of their communities, not to take responsibility away from them.

This is not an argument for returning to some idealised and nostalgic vision of a past era, or for abandoning a professional community services sector. It is rather a plea, before it is too late, for the sector to re-imagine its place within, and connection to, the broader community where organisations rediscover and reinvigorate their mission as the means for harnessing the generosity and creativity of their local communities, rather than simply as contractors to government.

At the heart of such an endeavour must be the commitment to a new community development paradigm for the provision of our services. Such a model would both enthuse and rally local people, including local businesses, to discover together local solutions for vulnerable and marginalised people.

This is the challenge, and it is an urgent one: to begin now to

---

[71] For information on the Brotherhood of St Laurence, see www.bsl.org.au/about/our-history/; accessed on 1 July 2016.

change the very *modus operandi* of the community services network from possessing an expertise in the delivery of narrowly conceived services specified by government funders, to creatively building expertise in helping ordinary citizens to support their vulnerable neighbours and strengthen community life. Clearly there are pockets of such innovative community development approaches, but they are swimming against the tide. As a sector, community service providers need to rediscover the skills required to assist ordinary members of the community to provide basic services to strengthen community life. This could be by providing access to work experience and literacy and numeracy tutoring, supporting struggling parents, visiting the isolated and lonely, assisting in the community integration of the homeless and newly arrived, and much, much more.

The inability to meet present and emerging needs

Evidence exists, both here in Australia and internationally, that complex social ills can only be tackled successfully if they are tackled at the local level with the whole community involved. This can be achieved if services are delivered locally by organisations well embedded in the community. Many of them would be small. Significantly, this does not require the sacrifice of efficiency. Indeed, there are ways in which governments can support genuine local solutions while achieving a real impact. Such innovative funding and governance approaches that give primacy to local community initiatives do exist already.

However, two tendencies militate against such progress. The first is the acceptance, at least by government, that voluntary community agencies are an extension of government. Recent attempts at sector 'reform' are evidence of this mindset. Such efforts are less about genuine reform and more about government efforts to streamline the operations of the Department of Human Services by tightly prescribing service responses and maximising efficiencies and outcomes through economies of scale. Some government initiatives, such as the attempt to coordinate service delivery and reduce fragmentation, duplication and inefficiency through 'Services Connect', seem laudable but should not be confused with sector reform. It could only be so if one's starting point was to consider voluntary community organisations to be an extension of government rather than an extension of community. And it is disturbing how easy it is for the community services sector to think in this way and to embrace processes that consolidate this starting point. The sector must be sensitive to the danger such an understanding of identity might be in losing the sense of mission and clarity around the sector's purpose.

One fallout from entrenching the view that the sector is an arm of government rather than of the community, whether intended or not, is the creation of an environment, over time, that is driving many organisations to amalgamate in order to survive. Small is no longer beautiful.

If the trajectory of amalgamation of organisations continues unabated over the next twenty years, we may see a social services 'arms race' in which the lion's share of government funding will go to super-sized social services businesses, some of which will be 'for-profit', with smaller, community-based and faith-based organisations left to wither on the margins.

In this emerging world, huge not-for-profit organisations look suspiciously like similar sized for-profit organisations and some research suggests that the convergence of the two has already taken place in Australia's Job Services system. Why would governments not treat them equally? The final act of this scenario can be seen being played out in the United Kingdom Government's Job Programme, which is dominated by very large multinational companies with enormous financial backing able to bid the unit price down, take a dominant place in the market, and then pressure government to take a stick to the unemployed.

Both a self-understanding that comes to see the community services sector as an extension of government and a major consequence of this, the tendency towards amalgamating organisations into mega-agencies to attract more funding, inevitably lead to a loss of connection to community roots, a loss of community ownership of services and a diminishment of voluntary community involvement. In the world of contract service delivery, these are considered externalities worthy of little consideration.

However, if it is true, as stated above, that the most effective way of addressing complex social needs is by tackling them at the local level with extensive community contribution, then it becomes imperative that the sector pull back and begin again to re-imagine how it might harness community goodwill and creativity to build community strength and wellbeing into the future. For indeed, if the contention being affirmed here about the unsustainability of the current paradigm is proved correct, then it is these very local services with the capacity to garner community contributions and support that will be needed to see us into the future.

Re-orientating the community services sector/government relationship

There is an emerging consensus that the community services sector, which in Australia originated not in government but in the community itself, motivated by moral rather than economic or managerial imperatives, is being stripped of its ethos of service to the community and its ethic of voluntarism. The contracting ethic, which has become dominant under governments of all political colours, is increasingly seen as a drain on the sector's moral energy and enthusiasm.

However, what is being suggested here, that there is an urgent need to reimagine the community services sector and its relationship both to local community and to government, should not be mistaken for a call for the withdrawal of government. On the contrary, the critical role of governments, both state and national, to fund pivotal social infrastructure such as health, education, housing and income support provisions, is acknowledged. Such commitment from governments is required to ensure the human dignity and quality of life of all members of society.

The reimagining of the sector which is envisaged is rather a new and creative model that more effectively harnesses the different areas of expertise of both government and the local community and reflects more accurately the realities that our society will face in the decades ahead. Such a model might include the following components:

- Governance and accountability for community welfare outcomes would be devolved significantly to local communities with financial support for services channelled through a coordinating non-government organisation. In this area, recent thinking, such as the concept of 'collective impact' from the United States of America[72] or the idea of 'mass localism' from the United Kingdom,[73] has much to offer us.

- The key focus of the community building effort and voluntary contribution will be on prevention and early intervention. On the other hand, the energies of paid service delivery professionals would be directed to the 'high needs' end of the continuum of individual and family problems where they may also be supported by volunteers.

- An 'all of community' response to local needs would be driven by a systemic and collaborative effort on the part of sector organisations which would inform the community and encourage activism.

- Whilst the sector workforce would consist of a smaller proportion of paid staff, they would broadly fall into three categories: firstly, those with expertise in community-building, fostering community activism and supporting volunteers; secondly, those with broad service delivery skills who would not be constrained by adherence to one service delivery model; and thirdly, a small group of practitioners who would provide highly skilled interventions and secondary consultation.

- Professional practice would be significantly re-oriented towards building the capacities and material resources of individuals, families and the community and, for this reason, the training of staff would be geared towards community

---

[72] Collective Impact is a framework for collaboration between government, business, philanthropy, not-for-profits and citizens to tackle deeply entrenched and complex social problems to achieve lasting change; accessed on 1 July 2016 at www.collaborationforimpact.com/collective-impact/.

[73] For information on mass localism, see L. Bunt and M. Harris, 2010. *Mass Localism: A Way to Help Small Communities Solve Big Social Challenges*. London: NESTA; accessed on 1 July 2016 at www.nesta.org.uk/publications/mass-localism.

engagement, community development and a range of cross-disciplinary skills.

Far from exhaustive, these suggestions are a beginning and, notwithstanding an appreciation of the enormous task of re-imagining and re-orientating the sector and the challenges entailed, begin we must.

Mission-Inspired Responses to a Changing Environment

Ricki Jeffrey

Introduction

In 2009 Centacare*CQ* (Centacare Central Queensland) reimagined a better way of responding as a Church agency to its mission. Since that time Centacare*CQ* has taken a strategic and intentional focus on sharing in the healing ministry of Jesus with its staff. This means that significant work has been undertaken to educate and inform staff about the importance of mission to the organisation, but even more importantly staff have been on a journey of discovery and empowerment as they have realised real life examples of how each day at the coal face is an opportunity for them to share Jesus' love through their ministry. This paper presents an approach to an integrated understanding of 'mission in practice' that seeks to be cogent and theologically informed. This approach takes the position that, in Catholic agencies, Catholic identity should be observable and witnessed by staff and those whom they serve and that the mission is foundational to all actions.

In the Centacare*CQ* experience the predominant challenges to upholding this position have been the influences of the changing paradigms of economics and workforce, both of which will be briefly explained through a 'potted history' of the origins and growth of Centacare*CQ*. Although a specific case, Centacare*CQ*'s story is not dissimilar to those of other Catholic-based social service organisations. Its history shows a shift from the foundation years when services were funded by the diocese and service delivery was provided predominantly by religious and then Catholic laity to primarily government-funded services delivered by a workforce of diverse traditions. The Centacare*CQ* story demonstrates the impacts on mission, and the challenges for understanding, what mission looks like in every day actions in a community-based social services environment that has experienced these two significant shifts.

Mission and history

The healing ministry of Jesus is the foundation of Catholic-based social service organisations, as their roots are in outreach services to the poor and dispossessed that were provided by their founding parish or religious order for which the mission was the driver of all service delivery. Over time there has been a decline in the explicit understanding that mission is the driver for the existence of such organisations and the services provided. There are a number of reasons for this, although without doubt a major factor is the decision by these organisations to broaden their capabilities through accessing government funding and government funding bodies demanding pluralistic and non-denominational services. As this shift occurred CentacareCQ, like so many other organisations of its type, has been faced for some time with the seemingly "inescapable tension" of "playing both sides of the street", that is, of satisfying both Government requirements and its own mission imperatives.[74]

Today, for many agencies, the funding source to carry out the healing ministry of Jesus has shifted almost entirely from the founding diocese or religious order, and at the same time, for many of our organisations, Catholic identity and mission as foundational to all actions have diminished. It would seem that systems, goals and purposes are focussed on business, especially business on behalf of the government, and that this can be at the expense of mission, which in turn has affected agencies' structures and interrelationships.[75] In the case of CentacareCQ, although such a 'handover of mission' to receive more and more government funds was not intentional, it was the cause of a mission fracture, as it has been in many faith-based social services organisations.

Parallel with the changing funding environment was a shift in the nature of the workforce from originally predominantly religious and then Catholic laity to one with more diverse traditions and, in fact, to workforces which are multi-racial, multi-ethnic and multi-faith.

---

[74] F. Quinlan, 2008. 'Common Challenges for Health, Education and Social Services', in N. Ormerod (ed.) *Identity and Mission in Catholic Agencies*. Strathfield, NSW: St Pauls Publications, pp. 39-58, see p. 48.

[75] P. Werhane, 'Moral Imagination and Systems Thinking', *Journal of Business Ethics*, 2002, 38, 32-42.

When mission was not an explicit feature of corporate statements for CentacareCQ, there was a period in its history when staff were not consciously aware of, or able to articulate or even demonstrate, mission in their daily work activities.

CentacareCQ's roots were definitely driven by mission as, although not founded by a religious order, it grew out of the Christian Family Centre established in the late 1970s by Fr Frank Gilbert (a Diocesan Priest) and Sr Anne Marie Kinnane (a Sister of Mercy) to offer counselling and relationship services, particularly natural family planning, to regional and rural parishioners who were not able to access these supports in other ways. From its humble beginnings working from a small 'donga' (temporary accommodation) in Rockhampton, in 2016 CentacareCQ has sites in Blackwater, Emerald, Gladstone, Longreach, Mackay, Rockhampton and Yeppoon, a catchment area of approximately 588,586 square kilometres or 32.7 percent of the state of Queensland. Services delivered include counselling, employee assistance programs, community education, family support, intensive child supports, domestic and family violence work, family dispute resolution, community aged care, mental health and disability support services, natural family planning, pre-marriage education and a range of short-term government-funded services such as drought support and flood recovery programs. The funding of CentacareCQ has moved from a small budget financed entirely by the Diocese to currently receiving $17 million annually from a range of federal and state government departments. The initiative in the 1970s to support the community of Rockhampton, and later Central Queensland, was grounded in a commitment to justice, Gospel values and the call to the mission, "to share in the healing ministry of Jesus by providing professional community services to enhance the wellbeing of individuals and families".[76]

The mission has always sat at the centre of the agency's work, however inevitably there have been a variety of interpretations applied to that mission over the last 42 years as the organisation has grown, staff composition has become much more diverse, and there has been less direct involvement with clergy and religious.

---

[76] CentacareCQ, 2016. *About Us – Mission, Vision & Values*. Rockhampton: Centacare; accessed on 4 April 2016 at www.centacare.net/index.php/about-us/mission-vision-a-values.

Re-establishing a focus on mission

In 2009 CentacareCQ began to explore its current workforce's understanding of how the mission was lived and enacted. In a section of the annual staff survey that year, which sought to identify understanding and demonstration of the mission, responses reflected a high level of agreement with the statements presented and a consistent but very low level of disagreement. Notable, however, was the level of neutral responses. "By their nature, such responses are given for various reasons, but despite this, the level of response could have inferred that some staff members do not reflect upon these matters as being significant enough to warrant consideration".[77] In fact, there was little sense that their work stemmed from a personal obligation to be active and productive participants in the life of society.

Follow-up work from this survey was conducted to seek staff views about how, as individuals, they demonstrated mission in their work. There was a strong opinion among staff that mission was 'lived' through the 'way' care or service was provided and the single most definable feature that drove the work was an individual's 'passion', not mission. Although there were specific examples of evidence of 'living the mission', there were no links made to the ministry of Jesus or the principles of the Church's Social Teaching being articulated. Further, there was evidence that staff considered that their 'passion' was based on a notion that they were "making a gift of their possessions to the poor person. They were handing over what was theirs".[78]

At the level of governance, in 2010 CentacareCQ's constitution was reviewed by the then Bishop of Rockhampton, Brian Heenan, and one of the additions made to the constitution was "that all staff receive formation in gospel values and Catholic Social Teaching" (p. 3). This change also drove CentacareCQ's journey to address, with the diverse workforce, their understanding of mission in a Catholic context and to provide the discourse for understanding how mission operates effectively. The goal of this journey is captured in CentacareCQ's 2011-2014 Strategic Plan, namely "to increase recognition of Catholic Identity of CentacareCQ

---

[77] M. Fahl, 2009. *Centacare Staff Satisfaction Survey Report*. Rockhampton: Centacare, p. 2.
[78] D. Dorr, 1992. *Option for the Poor*. Collins. Dove: Blackburn, Victoria, p. 35.

and realise mission as foundational to all actions thus building strategic competence and strengthening organisational character" with the intent that the mission-margin struggle would be once more "a life giving one".[79]

The indicator for the measurement of success of the strategic goal was the increased "articulation of how gospel values and core principles of Catholic Social Teaching inform practice" (CentacareCQ 2011-2014 Strategic Plan). Whilst a strategic goal for 2014 had been established, it was thought important to align the timelines for this piece of work with other planned significant changes that were being undertaken in the organisation. So as for other planning tasks, the question "What does the organisation need to have in place by 2020 so that mission is foundation to all our actions?" was addressed. Basically it was agreed that "three things had to be achieved:

- leadership that is observably Mission driven;
- staff gaining confidence in their understanding of and talking about Mission;
- culture of listening and responding so that we were facilitative of Mission".[80]

When choosing a starting point, it became obvious that Catholic identity and mission as foundational to all actions does not come across as something 'packaged' that can be easily taken up by a diverse workforce nor is institutional identity something 'possessed'. CentacareCQ is, therefore, working to build an understanding that Catholic identity and mission are both constant and unfolding to assist staff to connect their everyday work at CentacareCQ to its Catholic identity in a way that is observable and witnessed by staff and to ensure that the mission is foundational to all actions. Thus, CentacareCQ's current strategic intent is to create a culture "in which employees became partners in [the] enterprise" of the mission and leadership is clearly aligned with that mission so that work

---

[79] D. Ready, 'How Story Telling Builds Next Generation Leaders', *MIT Sloan Management Review*, 2002, Summer, 63-69.
[80] R. Jeffery and K. Venables, 2011. *Centacare Mission Program Logic 2011-2014*. Rockhampton: Centacare.

"flows directly from our mission" and staff are "transparent in their own accountability for the mission entrusted to them".[81]

By 2012 CentacareCQ had adopted the parable of the Good Samaritan (*Luke* 10:29-37) as an explicit way to identify mission as a living reality in relationships with clients. The parable was chosen as it exemplifies the work of the social services sector in that it begins with the vulnerable and disempowered who often are abandoned by their aggressors and other parts of society. In this parable the horror of formally being made unclean makes the priest and Levite turn away (*Luke* 10:31-32). Whilst the behaviour of the priest and Levite has no resonance for many of those who work in CentacareCQ, the action of the Samaritan does, as it seems to apply directly to their experience of triaging clients in times of need and crisis and then, as was the case with the Samaritan engaging the innkeeper, organising appropriate referrals to other supports in the wider community. The strengths-based perspective of this parable reflects the CentacareCQ practice framework of working with clients and enabling them to grow and flourish in their communities.

In 2012 CentacareCQ conducted a staff faith identity survey and despite 49 percent of the workforce identifying as Catholic, it was clear that the significant majority of staff were not able to name the principles of Catholic Social Teaching in terms any more specific than "helping others without judgement", "supporting those who can't support themselves" and "aiding people who no-one else will help".[82] The notions of human dignity, the common good, solidarity and subsidiarity were not made explicit. Thus, notwithstanding that the language of mission and values by now appeared to be entrenched in organisational documents, employee contracts, codes of conduct and ethics, training etc., an articulation of mission being foundational to all actions was not entrenched in this workforce. There was still a way to go in order to effect the desired transformation as documented in the strategy for change.

In 2013 CentacareCQ launched a mandatory staff formation program, Mission Matters. In order to make scripture accessible to all and to provide an effective tool to which staff could connect their everyday

---

[81] B. Yanofchick, 'Servant Leadership', *Health Progress*, September/October 2007, 88(5), 6-7.
[82] K. Venables, 2012. *Faith Identity Survey Report*. Rockhampton: Centacare.

work, a very informal and often colloquial turn of phrase was applied as the approach to teach that mission is foundational to all actions and that Catholic identity must be observable and witnessed by staff and clients. Thus, a colloquial story telling genre was adopted initially to expose staff to Gospel teachings; it involved reflecting weekly on the Sunday Gospel reading, putting the message of the Gospel into the contemporary context of CentacareCQ, and issuing a call to action to staff based on the message of the reading.

It was tempting to dilute the 'Catholicness' of our roots, as presumably this would have been an easier path. CentacareCQ, however, opted not to take that path when developing its formation program, which addresses mission, Gospel values and Catholic Social Teaching, without shying away from the actual words of the Gospel and the explicit use of 'Jesus' and 'God'.

Once this approach was accepted in the workforce, it was then taken to another level and used to develop an understanding of the four main principles of Catholic Social Teaching: the dignity of the human person, the common good, solidarity and subsidiarity. The colloquial story telling explicated each principle in a three-step process; what it is, how we do it and how we can do it better. Staff can now articulate that they do not work just for pay or rewards, rather they consciously respond to the humanity and dignity of the other. At the coalface, when staff talk to unhappy clients, when they are mediating or counselling a feuding family, or when they care for another of their team, they are embodying the core principle of dignity of the human person. Likewise, the principle of solidarity can be evidenced when staff provide that little extra service for clients, set up safe spaces for those who are unsafe, or reschedule aspects of their lives to provide services in a crisis.

Conclusion

As CentacareCQ's recent history highlights, relying on government funding sources can be associated with organisational development in a way that poses significant challenges to keeping mission explicit. So too can a diverse and pluralistic workforce which needs to be influenced to 'buy in' to a 'willingness to work for mission' in the sense of the Catholic tradition. If Catholic organisations want their distinctive feature to be the mission, then every opportunity must be taken to bring the scriptures and the social teachings of the Church into 'dialogue' with the workforce. The scriptures and Catholic Social Teaching need to be connected and couched in everyday terms to give mission 'life' in Catholic organisations. As the journey of mission rediscovery has been unfolding at CentacareCQ, there is evidence that there is a greater capacity for staff to name who God is and what God does – and to "recognise their own capacity to be Jesus for others".[83] An example of such evidence was witnessed at a recent Direct Care Worker meeting when a staff member linked work and scripture in this way:

> Jesus is speaking and he says: 'A new commandment I give unto you, that ye love one another; as I have loved you, that ye also love one another' (*John* 13:34).
>
> To be sharing in Jesus' ministry we need to show this love to our clients, whoever they are, whatever their needs. Through all the changes that are occurring in the industry, it is important that we maintain our caring and continue to support our clients by taking time to complete the jobs that they think are important. (CentacareCQ staff member)

This example shows that Catholic identity can indeed be observable and witnessed by staff. Another example of staff seeing mission as foundational to all actions is an outcome of an internal working group's development of CentacareCQ's Customer Service Model. This model has mission accountability at its centre and a set of key performance indicators matched to that accountability. Both examples demonstrate articulation of the re-alignment of mission and business so that the mission is being seen as foundational to our work and once again becoming "the senior partner driving or permeating *all* decisions in the business side".[84]

---

[83] C. Caldwell, R.D. Dixon, L.A. Floyd, J. Chaudoin, J. Post and G. Cheokas, 'Transformative Leadership: Achieving Unparalleled Excellence', *Journal of Business Ethics*, 2012, 109, 175 -187.

[84] G.A. Arbuckle, 2007. *Crafting Catholic Identity in Postmodern Australia*. Canberra: Catholic Health Australia, p. 84.

Mission Making a Difference:

Responses to Vulnerable People

Making a Real Difference to Poverty

Marcelle Mogg

Together with my colleagues in the Catholic social services sector, I draw renewed courage and hope from the words and actions of Pope Francis in calling the Church to stand again with people made vulnerable. There are two quotes from Pope Francis that have particularly captured my attention. They speak of links between the heart of mercy, the theological concept of jubilee, and the hard data that shows the reality of many Australian communities who are stuck in cycles of poverty:

> The time has come for the Church to take up the joyful call to mercy once more. It is time to return to the basics and to bear the weaknesses and struggles of our brothers and sisters. Mercy is the force that reawakens us to new life and instils in us the courage to look to the future with hope.[85]

> It is my burning desire that, during this Jubilee, the Christian people may reflect on the *corporal and spiritual works of mercy*. It will be a way to reawaken our conscience, too often grown dull in the face of poverty.[86]

The extraordinary Jubilee Year of Mercy captures the deep longing for a reset whereby those who have been excluded can re-enter all aspects of society, where the effects of economic and social exclusion are not perpetuated in the next generation.

The picture of entrenched disadvantage illustrated in the *Dropping Off The Edge 2015* report[87] shows clearly that a new way to address individual

---

[85] Pope Francis, 2015. *Misericordiae Vultus:* Bull of Indiction of the Extraordinary Jubilee of Mercy. Vatican: Vatican City, Section 10; accessed on 13 April 2016 at w2.vatican.va.
[86] Ibid., Section 15.
[87] T. Vinson and M. Rawsthorne with A. Beavis and M. Ericson, 2015. *Dropping Off The Edge 2015: Persistent Communal Disadvantage in Australia.* Melbourne and Canberra: Jesuit Social Services and Catholic Social Services Australia; accessed on 13 April 2016 at www.dote.org.au.

and community disadvantage is needed. The report highlights a point in time for Australian communities, when those called to the social service ministries of the Catholic Church need to join together in order to focus their collective efforts to serve those living in the most disadvantaged communities, working with them to create a more life-giving future.

Addressing poverty

In seeking to address the structures of poverty in our communities and ameliorate their impact in the lives of those affected, those of us working in Catholic social services recognise that we must centre our efforts on the Gospel, acknowledging our own humanity and poverty, and that all of us are made whole only in Christ.

Dropping Off The Edge 2015 is more than social research and the communities the report identifies are not just indicators or rankings. *Dropping Off The Edge 2015* tells the story of the impact of the complex interplay of factors that trap people and whole communities in situations of disadvantage. The report helps us to understand the day-to-day challenges people face in trying to live in these communities. As Pope Francis reminds us, an authentic preferential option for the poor is not just a theology or a commitment to charitable activities or programs, but it is an active outworking of the vision of the Kingdom of God.

In particular, workshops entitled 'Making a Real Difference to Poverty', offered at the February 2016 Catholic Social Services conference,[88] provided time and space for us to reflect on what the *Dropping Off The Edge 2015* story means to those working in social service ministries.

The role of Catholic Social Services Australia

Catholic Social Services Australia sponsored the *Dropping Off The Edge 2015* report with Jesuit Social Services. This study was important to us as Catholic Social Services Australia, like Jesuit Social Services, works for

---

[88] The Catholic social services conference, *Review, Re-imagine, Renew: Mission making a difference in a changing world*, where the workshops were offered and which inspired this volume, was held in Melbourne on 24-26 February 2016.

a fairer, more inclusive Australian society that reflects and supports the dignity and equality of all people. We know that people who experience entrenched disadvantage can be disconnected from the social and economic opportunities which would enable them to participate in the life of the community and realise their own 'fullness of life'. Catholic Social Services Australia works to transform the structural causes of entrenched disadvantage and promote the increased wellbeing of those experiencing poverty. In this way we stand with our Catholic social service members who work alongside people affected by poverty and disadvantage.

Those involved in the work of transforming individual lives, families and communities recognise that inadequate income and unemployment are among the major factors that underpin entrenched disadvantage. Therefore the pursuit of the common good, through advocacy for social and economic policies that prioritise the social and economic wellbeing of those who are most disadvantaged, forms the basis for Catholic Social Services Australia's work.

Dropping Off The Edge 2015

The *Dropping Off The Edge 2015* research is the fruit of a partnership between Catholic Social Services Australia and Jesuit Social Services. Both Catholic Social Services Australia and Jesuit Social Services have a long history of working with vulnerable people and communities and advocating for better social and economic outcomes. *Dropping Off The Edge 2015* was authored by Professor Tony Vinson and Associate Professor Margot Rawsthorne from the University of Sydney, and is the fourth in a series of reports on disadvantage in Australia begun by Professor Vinson in 1999.

The aim of *Dropping Off The Edge 2015* was to have an up-to-date evidence base that supports advocacy efforts to improve the opportunities for communities experiencing entrenched disadvantage. This work is highly regarded across all groups involved in social welfare, from government to community groups. The research makes a substantial contribution to the current national dialogue on inequality and the effects of poverty and unemployment in limiting the lives of Australians.

Dropping Off The Edge 2015 maps disadvantage in each postcode area, by analysing 22 variables that are recognised internationally as indicators of disadvantage (see Table 1).

Table 1 – Indicators of disadvantage

Variable name	Description of indicator of disadvantage
Internet access	Proportion of households without access to the internet
Housing stress	Proportion of households allocating 30% or more of income to housing costs
Low family income	Proportion of households with an income less than $600 per week
Overall education	Proportion of the population aged 16-65 years who left school before 15 years of age
Post-schooling qualifications	Proportion of population aged 18-64 years not possessing degree/diploma/graduate diploma/graduate certificate/postgraduate degree/certificate
Unskilled workers	Proportion of the workforce (ABS definition)* classified as lowest skill (ABS definition)
Young adults not engaged	Proportion of 17-24 year olds neither engaged in full-time study nor work
Readiness for schooling	Proportion of all children tested for language and cognitive skills (school-based) and assessed as being "developmentally vulnerable"
Disability Support	Proportion of people aged 18-64 years in receipt of the Disability Support Pension
Long-term unemployment	Proportion of the workforce (ABS definition) aged 18-64 years in receipt of Newstart for one year or more
Rent assistance	Proportion of people aged 18 and over in receipt of rental assistance
Unemployment	Proportion of the workforce (ABS definition) aged 18-64 years in receipt of Newstart
Y3 numeracy	Proportion of year 3 students not "At or Above National Minimum Standard Percentage" on the numeracy assessment scales
Y3 reading	Proportion of year 3 students not "At or Above National Minimum Standard Percentage" on the reading assessment scales

* For details of ABS definitions, see the Australian Bureau of Statistics (ABS) website; accessed on 13 April 2016 at www.abs.gov.au.

Variable name	Description of indicator of disadvantage
Y9 numeracy	Proportion of year 9 students not "At or Above National Minimum Standard Percentage" on the numeracy assessment scales
Y9 reading	Proportion of year 9 students not "At or Above National Minimum Standard Percentage" on the reading assessment scales
Child maltreatment	Rate of confirmed maltreatment of a child per 1,000 children and young people under 15 years of age
Criminal convictions	Rate per 1,000 of people aged 18-49 years convicted of crime
Juvenile convictions	Rate per 1,000 of people 10-17 years convicted or found guilty of crime
Domestic violence	Rate of domestic/family violence orders per 1,000 of the population aged 18-64 years
Prison admissions	Rate per 1,000 of people aged 18-49 years admitted to prison
Psychiatric admissions	Rate of psychiatric hospital admissions per 1,000 of the population over 18 years of age

The final report, including an analysis of the findings, state-based reports, tables with rankings and maps, is available at the *Dropping Off The Edge 2015* website – www.DOTE.org.au.

The analysis of the indicators showed that a small number of communities across Australia carry the burden of disadvantage across multiple indicators, with disproportionately high levels of unemployment, low family income and education, housing stress, domestic violence, and prison admissions. These factors combine to create severe limitations on the opportunities in life for children, adults and communities, which in turn generate significant social and economic costs for the broader community.

A major finding of the report is the consistency with which localities identified as being extremely disadvantaged in 2015 resemble those similarly ranked in earlier studies. The report shows that, during the 15-year period that Professor Vinson and his team have researched this issue, the vast majority of the most disadvantaged communities continue to bear the social and economic burden of entrenched deprivation.

How can we make a real difference to poverty?

Since *Dropping Off The Edge 2015* was released in July 2015, Catholic Social Services Australia and Jesuit Social Services have conducted state briefings and stakeholder workshops across the country. Over 400 people have attended, from governments, including politicians and departmental staff, and people working in the community and private sectors. The breadth of interest shows that there remains among ordinary Australians a desire to confront the issues that perpetuate disadvantage.

In addition, the opportunity to facilitate workshops at the 2016 *Review, Reimagine, Renew* conference, provided a significant space for people committed to Catholic social services to reflect on what the evidence means for our areas of ministry. In these sessions there was a sense of energy as people drawn together by our shared mission saw the potential for creative partnerships across all parts of the Catholic Church, from education, health, social services, parish ministries and research agencies, to work with communities experiencing disadvantage to seek to break free from the social and economic factors that limit people's lives.

The themes emerging from these conversations were consistent with reflections from the broader workshops conducted nationally. The opportunities to hear from people involved in breaking cycles of poverty contribute to a greater understanding of entrenched disadvantage, and to identifying what works at a local level and, most importantly, what is hindering communities from experiencing social transformation. Most participants were optimistic, sharing stories of where change has occurred. However, there was some frustration that, although the solutions to overcoming entrenched disadvantage are often well researched and widely known, current policy settings and funding models do not facilitate the long-term commitment required to enable programs and support initiatives to take effect. Overcoming the degree of social disadvantage identified requires change that is sustained across a generation, not a term of government.

A number of overarching common themes have emerged.

1. Local context does matter

Too often we heard that funding was not wisely spent and services were not targeted to the needs of the local community. There were also many stories about duplication of services, competition amongst service providers that mitigate the effectiveness of support strategies, and short term responses.

Across Australia, communities are dealing with vastly diverse social and economic issues and this is borne out by the data collected in *Dropping Off The Edge*. Local community issues and needs have not always been well understood by those making policy and funding decisions. This has been due to limited consultation by relevant authorities, a general disregard for the solution to emerge from within the community, a lack of robust and appropriate data, and no apparent lead agency.

Many workshop participants spoke about the positive role that local governments, regional coordinating bodies or 'community hubs' can have in being the voice for the local community and coordinating action. This reflects the reality that the factors that contribute to entrenched disadvantage are locational. For this reason, decision making and responses to disrupt cycles of disadvantage must be based on the principle of subsidiarity, and be made and coordinated locally.

There was a unanimous plea for state, territory and federal levels of government to be cognisant of local needs and community factors when determining priorities. This could also include strengthening the approach to planning and allocation of funding by understanding the social and health needs of communities and, in particular, linking the evidence of the determinants of health with the indicators of disadvantage.

It was also recognised that, over time, changes in the issues affecting specific communities can impact on the degree of disadvantage experienced by communities. For example, in South Australia there is expected to be a major loss of manufacturing jobs which will impact on the labour market, the economy and families. In another illustration, many participants related that the recent trend in availability and usage of the drug 'ice' is quickening the trajectory into entrenched disadvantage, particularly for young people.

Although *Dropping Off The Edge 2015* highlights the most disadvantaged communities in Australia, workshop participants also spoke of the 'hidden poor' in gentrified areas. Whilst *Dropping Off The Edge 2015* looks at evidence at the postcode level, the authors acknowledge that smaller areas of disadvantage can also be present in more highly advantaged areas. It is important that we do not lose sight of what is happening in each community.

2. Strong communities can ameliorate disadvantage

Communities that are cohesive, have visible and strong leaders, and have a vision for their community, fare better in addressing disadvantage and are more resilient. It was acknowledged that these are not the only contributors to success, and supporting services are also needed. However, strong communities can harness the resources of the business sector, education and employment opportunities, and draw on their sense of solidarity to represent their concerns to government better.

Some communities lack leadership and drive due to sustained economic and social hardship, or a lack of cohesive community groups. These communities need support but may not have a strong or articulate voice into government to lobby for assistance. However, it was felt that the value of investment in community leadership and development was often overlooked by governments.

Participants spoke of the impact of shifting funding, in more recent times, away from 'community hub' models towards a single service and individualised services approach (such as the National Disability Insurance Scheme). As funding for activities such as community development has been reduced by governments, the perception grows that community development is not considered to be important or effective in addressing disadvantage. This funding divide between individualised service models and community-strengthening approaches potentially pitches one model of support against the other, lessening the effectiveness of both. A more holistic approach to breaking cycles of entrenched disadvantage would include location-based funding for support and community development, funding for universal services including early intervention, and individualised funding for services enabling people to choose the services that they most need. Funding commitments for programs designed to overcome disadvantage need to be for the long term. It may take more than a generation to see the fruit of the investment.

A strong theme to emerge from community consultations was the importance of all individuals and communities being valued by the broader Australian society. Participants working with members of such communities particularly spoke of the harm of labelling, blaming and victimising individuals and communities experiencing disadvantage. Some people involved in the Catholic social services sector spoke of the danger of assuming that disadvantaged communities do not have strong social cohesion or strong community relationships. The reality is that such communities, and particularly Indigenous communities, may well have strong community relationships.

In releasing *Dropping Off The Edge 2015*, the authors and sponsors were conscious that the information contained in the research could be used to either assist and empower, or to degrade and diminish individuals and communities. This is particularly pertinent in Australia today where governments and the media seek to limit the inherent value of people to their economic contribution to the wider community. This philosophy has the effect of undermining the human value and dignity of those individuals and communities who are excluded from economic participation due to lack of employment and education opportunities.

3. Rural and regional communities are impacted by the level of services and economic opportunities

Dropping Off The Edge 2015 identified a greater burden of disadvantage in regional and remote areas of Australia relative to urban communities. The research data were supported by the local consultations that Catholic Social Services Australia conducted in communities across Australia in both major cities and rural and regional areas, and by participants in the workshops at the 2016 *Review, Reimagine, Renew* conference.

In particular, there was concern about the lack of economic opportunities in many smaller communities which led to social problems such as long-term unemployment and youth disengagement. New ways of finding economic engagement were discussed, such as social enterprises and local businesses suitable for the area. However, many communities in the areas consulted were also resilient and had dealt with considerable community change. Workshop participants reiterated the observation that communities with strong leaders were better placed to tackle entrenched issues of disadvantage.

Issues in remote Indigenous communities were acknowledged as presenting distinctive challenges due to a lack of infrastructure and geographic isolation.

Conclusion

The conversations facilitated through the workshops, including those held at the 2016 *Review, Reimagine, Renew* conference, provided important directions and ideas for future action by government, the community, business and particularly those of us called to the ministry of social service. We all have a role, whether through advocacy based on evidence such as that provided by *Dropping Off The Edge 2015*, creative partnerships with like-minded agencies, or enabling the stories of the people affected by entrenched disadvantage to be heard.

The reflections from the workshops affirm Catholic Social Services Australia's advocacy position which has been formed from our conviction that these disadvantaged communities need to be part of a new Australian story. Catholic Social Services Australia calls for action in four main areas:

1. sustained and long-term commitment to change by all governments and across political parties;
2. addressing economic and social disadvantage at the individual, community and macro levels;
3. developing local solutions that are targeted, tailored and agile in responding to changes in community needs; and
4. integrating government services to support local solutions and effectively drive change.

Those of us compelled by Christ's love for the poor and the mandate of the social service ministries of the Church cannot and should not turn away from addressing the challenge of persistent and entrenched disadvantage. We must be people of hope, working to ensure that those living in communities affected by long-term poverty will have opportunities to thrive. We must also be willing to see the potential that we have within our own Church to foster creative and energetic partnerships so that hope is translated into new stories of communal flourishing. This is a particular imperative in the Jubilee Year of Mercy.

Putting Child Safety First

Gerard Jones and Ché Stockley

Context

In recent years inquiries in a range of jurisdictions have highlighted organisational failures to protect children and young people. Community pressure on governments and associated institutions has resulted in dedicated police investigations, parliamentary inquiries and judicial inquiries. Irenyi *et al* note the common thread running through the Senate inquiries, *Bringing Them Home* (1997), *Lost Innocents* (2001) and *Forgotten Australians* (2004)[89] was that abuse has been a feature of institutional practices of the 19th and 20th centuries and that such practices still occur.[90]

---

[89] Human Rights and Equal Opportunity Commission, 1997. *Bringing Them Home: Report of the National Inquiry into the Separation of Aboriginal and Torres Strait Islander Children from their Families*; www.humanrights.gov.au/publications/bringing-them-home-report-1997; Senate Community Affairs References Committee Secretariat, 2001. *Lost Innocents: Righting the record – Report on child migration*; www.aph.gov.au/Parliamentary_Business/Committees/Senate/Community_Affairs/Completed_inquiries/1999-02/child_migrat/report/index; and Senate Community Affairs References Committee Secretariat, 2004. *Forgotten Australians: A report on Australians who experienced institutional or out-of-home care as children*; www.aph.gov.au/Parliamentary_Business/Committees/Senate/Community_Affairs/Completed_inquiries/2004-07/inst_care/report/index, respectively. Canberra: Commonwealth of Australia; accessed on 10 May 2016.

[90] M. Irenyi, L. Bromfield, L. Beyer and D. Higgins, 2006. 'Child maltreatment in organisations: Risk factors and strategies', *Child Abuse Prevention Issues*, No. 25, Spring.

A sharper focus on this problem has been provided by the Victorian Parliamentary Inquiry into the Handling of Child Abuse by Religious and Other Organisations (2012-2013) and the Royal Commission into Institutional Responses to Child Sexual Abuse (commenced in 2013).[91]

The report of the Victorian Parliamentary Inquiry into the Handling of Child Abuse by Religious and Other Organisations called *Betrayal of Trust* was tabled in November 2013.[92] This report examined the deficiencies in child protection in Victoria and advocated for systems reform. The report emphasised the need for increased responsibilities for the formal oversight of child safety in organisations and the introduction of a requirement for early education and community service organisations to meet a minimum standard for ensuring a child safe environment and a zero tolerance approach to criminal child abuse.

In addition, findings and research as they incrementally emerge from the Royal Commission into Institutional Responses to Child Sexual Abuse have also focussed on the necessity of creating child safety within organisations.

Child safe frameworks

In the Royal Commission's consultation paper, *Institutional Responses to Child Sexual Abuse in Out-of-Home Care*,[93] the key elements of a child safe organisation are described as:

- organisational leadership, governance and culture,
- human resources management,
- child safe policies and procedures,

---

[91] For details of the Victorian Parliamentary Inquiry and Royal Commission, see respectively www.parliament.vic.gov.au/fcdc/inquiry/340 and www.childabuseroyalcommission.gov.au; accessed on 10 May 2016.

[92] Family and Community Development Committee, 2013. *Betrayal of Trust: Inquiry into the handling of child abuse by religious and other non-government organisations*. Melbourne: Parliament of Victoria.

[93] Royal Commission into Institutional Responses to Child Sexual Abuse (RCIRCSA), 2016. Consultation Paper: *Institutional Responses to Child Sexual Abuse in Out-of-Home Care*. Sydney: RCIRCSA; accessed on 10 May 2016 at www.childabuseroyalcommission. gov.au/getattachment/5caff916-1895-433e-a7f7-535e3f3e80df/Out-of-home-care-Consultation-Paper.

- education and training,
- children's participation and empowerment,
- family and community involvement,
- the organisation's physical and online environment,
- review and continuous improvement of policies and processes,
- child-focused complaint processes.

Through the consultation paper, the Royal Commission sought public comment on these elements and proposed a nationally consistent scheme.

Child safe schemes are now an accepted mechanism for protecting children and preventing abuse. A number of jurisdictions have commenced the work of creating child safe frameworks or incorporating child safe principles into existing systems of regulation and accreditation. While articulated differently, each of the approaches shares elements such as communicating the priority of child safety, practices for the screening, recruitment and supervision of volunteers, having clear and understood practices to manage and respond to the risk of child abuse, formally articulating and embedding the child safety-related expectations of staff and volunteers through codes of conduct, and ensuring the voice of children is heard and acted upon.

One such example is the NSW Office for the Children's Guardian guidelines, 'Become a Child Safe Organisation'.[94] Under these guidelines, an organisation demonstrating the key elements of child safe practice:

- develops child safe policies,
- has a child safe code of conduct,
- ensures effective staff recruitment and training,
- understands privacy considerations,
- has a plan for managing risk,

---

[94] For further information on 'Become a Child Safe Organisation', see www.kidsguardian.nsw.gov.au/working-with-children/child-safe-organisations/become-a-childsafe-organisation; accessed on 10 May 2016.

- encourages children and young people to participate,
- effectively deals with concerns or complaints about behaviours towards a child,
- attends child safe organisations' training.

Elements of a child safety framework

The Victorian government made a commitment to undertake a range of activities to respond to the recommendations of the *Betrayal of Trust* report. This included the introduction of Child Safe Standards in 2015.[95] The expectation was that organisations working with children will work towards compliance with the standards from 1 January 2016.

The Victorian Child Safety Standards are:
- strategies to embed an organisational culture of child safety, including through effective leadership arrangements,
- a Child Safe Policy or Statement of Commitment to Child Safety,
- a Code of Conduct that establishes clear expectations for appropriate behaviour with children,
- screening, supervision, training and other human resource practices that reduce the risk of child abuse by new and existing personnel,
- processes for responding to and reporting suspected child abuse,
- strategies to identify and reduce or remove risks of child abuse,
- strategies to promote the participation and empowerment of children.

---

[95] For information on the Child Safe Standards, see www.dhs.vic.gov.au/about-the-department/documents-and-resources/policies,-guidelines-and-legislation/child-safe-standards; accessed on 10 May 2016.

What MacKillop Family Services has done

At a simple level, the establishment of a child safe environment requires clear strategies, policies, procedures and practice coupled with the organisational conditions whereby these instruments will be prioritised and enacted. To this end, our agency, MacKillop Family Services,[96] has implemented the Sanctuary Model (see below) as an improved method of supporting the safety of children and enhanced existing processes that promote community safety.

Cultural change in organisations is critical to embracing child safety. Research conducted on behalf of the Royal Commission into Institutional Responses to Child Sexual Abuse has examined closely how communication failures occur and how this results in inaction when child abuse is suspected. As Munro and Fish acknowledge:

> Culture is partly created by explicit strategies and messages from senior managers but is also strongly influenced by the covert messages that run through the organisation and influence individual behaviour ... [W]orkers need not only a formal mechanism for making reports but some guidance on the threshold for action.[97]

The authors examined how the concepts of confirmation bias and representativeness heuristic operate to create organisational blindness to child abuse and prevent the flow of information which might allow child abuse to be identified promptly. For Munro and Fish a positive organisational culture is one in which staff are alert to suspicious behaviour and ready to share concerns.

The section following outlines how the Sanctuary Model has augmented our practice and assisted MacKillop in prioritising and enacting a culture of child safety.

---

[96] MacKillop Family Services was formed in 1997 by the Sisters of Mercy, the Christian Brothers and the Sisters of St Joseph and is a leading provider of integrated services to children, young people and families. For information on MacKillop Family Services, see www.mackillop.org.au/history; accessed on 10 May.

[97] E. Munro and S. Fish, 2015. *Hear no evil, see no evil: Understanding failure to identify and report child sexual abuse in institutional contexts*. Sydney: Royal Commission into Institutional Responses to Child Sexual Abuse.

Introducing the Sanctuary Model

The Seven Commitments of the Sanctuary Model[98] are democracy, social learning, emotional intelligence, growth and change, social responsibility, open communication and non-violence.

MacKillop adopted Sanctuary to improve outcomes for children and young people in out-of-home care and ensure organisational congruence in adopting a trauma-informed, therapeutic approach to interactions with our clients and among staff.

Former CEO Micaela Cronin pointed to two key factors in implementing Sanctuary at MacKillop. The first was the difficulty with safely managing challenging behaviours of young people in residential care; the second was staff turnover. Sanctuary was viewed as a potential response to these and other challenges. Through addressing these challenges by adopting Sanctuary, there was a view that it would also be possible to enhance child safety within the organisation. Safety is central to Sanctuary.

Understanding trauma involves the acknowledgement that the children and young people in MacKillop's care have experienced trauma in their lives and recognition of how this trauma contributes to behaviour. Further, the Sanctuary Model assists organisations to acknowledge that colleagues and others with whom we have contact at work may also have been exposed to trauma, stress or adversity and this will influence how they behave and how they react to client behaviour.

The shared language of safety informs the concepts of SELF: Safety, Emotions, Loss and Future, an organising structure for the way we approach our work. The SELF domains are the key for healing and exploring these together allows:

> clients, their families, and staff ... to embrace a shared, non-technical and non-pejorative language that allows them all to see the larger recovery process in perspective. The accessible language demystifies what sometimes is seen as confusing and even insulting clinical or psychological terminology ...[99]

---

[98] For information on the Sanctuary Model, see sanctuaryweb.com/TheSanctuaryModel/ComponentsoftheSanctuaryModel/SELF.aspx; accessed on 10 May 2016.
[99] Ibid.

The conceptual framework of the Sanctuary Model is further supported by the Sanctuary Toolkit, a range of practical tools and approaches used by staff to help us implement and operationalise Sanctuary.

Sanctuary and the concept of the child safe organisation

Staff at MacKillop have been able to create a unifying pathway for child safety through the implementation of Sanctuary. Importantly, the Sanctuary Model acknowledges that to thrive and grow we need to feel safe. This is especially so for people who have experienced violence and abuse. Individuals who have experienced violence are attuned to threats and, although it is always possible they will react to perceived threats, Sanctuary attempts to ensure that real threats do not exist.[100]

Sanctuary encourages organisations to ensure they are physically safe, psychologically safe, socially safe, morally safe and culturally safe for clients. For MacKillop, Sanctuary and the journey to becoming a child safe organisation have a number of common elements.

Using the Victorian Child Safe Standards[101] as a template, the sections to follow outline how the Sanctuary Model has been used to build capability and practice to improve child safety.

Victorian Child Safety Standard 1: Strategies to embed an organisational culture of child safety, including through effective leadership arrangements

The overarching purpose of the Sanctuary Model is to embed a positive organisational culture which is focussed on recognising and overcoming trauma. Through the commitments of democracy, social responsibility and open communication, Sanctuary fosters an environment in which leaders within an organisation can initiate discussions about the importance of child safety and also hear from clients and staff about their experiences and how to make things better.

Through the adoption of shared language, the organisation-wide

---

[100] Ibid. and S.L. Bloom and B. Farragher, 2013. *Restoring Sanctuary: A new operating system for trauma-informed systems of care.* New York: Oxford University Press.
[101] Child Safe Standards, op. cit.

implementation and maintenance of robust systems to protect children and young people can be supported at all levels of the organisation. Further, with the whole organisation understanding Sanctuary, it is simpler for the organisation to comprehend and acknowledge the importance of child safety.

The process of the Sanctuary's implementation was, in practice, a demonstration of how to lead effective change to make the language and practice of safety more explicit and overt in order to create safety for all clients.

Victorian Child Safety Standard 2: A Child Safe Policy or Statement of Commitment to Child Safety

Safety is central to the practice of the Sanctuary Model. All staff members who are trained in the model learn about the pervasive nature of trauma for both clients and staff members and critically its impact on the people with whom we work. Understanding trauma and the impact of abuse and neglect on the children who come into out-of-home care requires a commitment to child safety.

Growth and change enable organisations to be flexible and adopt new ways of working. Through its commitment to growth and change, MacKillop is engaged in ongoing development of policies and procedures that encourage improvement in practice. For example, MacKillop Family Services introduced a Client Rights Policy in 2013. The right to safety is a strong thread that runs through this document with the acknowledgement that, in providing services to vulnerable and disadvantaged children, young people, families and former residents of institutions run by the founding congregations, MacKillop recognises the importance of respecting and protecting individual rights. This document is currently under review to strengthen further the focus on child safety.

Victorian Child Safety Standard 3: A Code of Conduct that establishes clear expectations for appropriate behaviour with children

Setting the expectation for all members of an organisation to uphold a child safe environment is a key element of all child safe standards frameworks. MacKillop has zero tolerance for child abuse and actively promotes the expectation that everyone is responsible for the care and protection of the children within our organisation.

MacKillop's Code of Conduct is supported by a range of measures for staff and volunteers to prioritise the safety of children. For example, position descriptions include a focus on the Sanctuary Model and emphasise promoting safety and recovery from adversity through the active creation of a trauma-informed community.

Victorian Child Safety Standard 4: Screening, supervision, training and other human resource practices that reduce the risk of child abuse by new and existing personnel

MacKillop has robust and effective written procedures for recruitment, screening, training and supervision of staff and volunteers. Sanctuary is intended to create an organisational culture that places value on the experience of children and young people, and ensuring that appropriate staff are recruited, and staff are supervised and trained in how to work effectively with children and young people who have experienced trauma.

With its overt focus on safety and emotional intelligence, the Sanctuary Model facilitates practice that is more democratic, transparent and accountable. The further focus on open communication acts as an antidote to factors that inhibit staff from raising concerns or initiating 'difficult conversations'. These factors combine to ensure that staff are well supported and, in our view, good supervision and support for staff and effective human resources practices will build staff resilience.

Victorian Child Safety Standard 5: Processes for responding to and reporting suspected child abuse and *Victorian Child Safety Standard 6: Strategies to identify and reduce or remove risks of child abuse*

Alongside strong procedures that ensure staff are screened, trained and supervised, MacKillop has procedures that detail how to identify and manage risks to children and respond to or report suspected child abuse.

In the Sanctuary Model, the commitment to open communication is a mechanism that allows all staff members to confront openly the risks of harm to children in the organisation. Open communication supports staff to talk safely about concerns with peers, managers and organisational leaders to address the risk of drift in the adherence to clear professional boundaries or proper processes.

Victorian Child Safety Standard 7: Strategies to promote the participation and empowerment of children

Sanctuary is based on practising 'deep democracy'. Much of the Sanctuary literature focuses on what this means for staff in hierarchical organisations. For MacKillop, democracy is also about involving children and young people in decision making about their home and care. Sanctuary describes democracy as one of the hardest things to learn for staff and clients, noting that "... participatory, deeply democratic processes must be experienced and the skills required must be learned".[102] Children who have experienced abuse before coming into care need to develop skills to participate in a democratic environment that are in direct opposition to the skills they acquired growing up in abusive homes.[103]

Democracy in Sanctuary is about hearing the voices of those around us. This includes ensuring that children and young people have a say about their care, their homes and concerns that they may have. MacKillop facilitates this through the implementation of mechanisms such as Viewpoint, an online survey tool for children and young

---

[102] Sanctuary, op. cit.
[103] Bloom, S.L. and Farragher, B., op. cit., p. 114.

people in care, and Youth Advisory Groups. Youth Advisory Groups are meetings held with senior staff members in which young people in residential care can talk about their home and the staff and other people around them in a manner that is safe and supported, and leads to concrete action.

Challenges for implementation

As noted by Munro and Fish, "establishing good policies, providing good training and creating a constructive organisational culture does not mean the job is done and senior managers can relax".[104] Changing staff culture to create a child safe organisation creates enormous challenges.

Engagement of staff and volunteers across the organisation has to be high to ensure that culture shift is possible. To implement Sanctuary at MacKillop an in-depth strategy was required including the provision of three days training to all of our 800-plus staff as well as a range of other implementation activities.

Significantly, implementing child safe standards may be viewed as another compliance mechanism for staff members who are already managing a range of compliance activities associated with their day-to-day work with children and young people.

Conclusion

To create a child safe environment requires ongoing action across many domains of organisational activity.

MacKillop's dual track approach of implementing the Child Safety Standards and the Sanctuary Model has positioned the organisation well to meet the challenges of providing an environment that is child safe. This approach has facilitated compliance with mandated standards within a cultural change that facilitates sustainability and an organisation-wide commitment.

As Catholic social services and the Church move to implement

---

[104] Munro, E. and Fish, S., op. cit.

improved practices for care of children and vulnerable people in light of the findings of the Royal Commission into Institutional Responses to Child Sexual Abuse, our approach to build a child safe environment provides an exemplar for consideration by other Church agencies.

Challenges in Advocacy and Support for Recently Arrived Refugees

Tomasa Morales

Setting the scene

Leaving everything behind to start a new life in a completely different country, where everything is new, is a challenge in itself. Starting a new life somewhere that has different laws and regulations to those with which you are accustomed, having to learn a new language, having to adapt to these new laws and culture is overwhelming and stressful. Appropriate settlement services can assist with many of these transitions. If such services are not accessible right after arrival, the delays can cause a number of issues for newly arrived refugees.

For most newly arrived refugees, making a new start is made more difficult due to the circumstances under which they left their homeland. Fleeing war zones and leaving loved ones behind can lead to the development of mental illness due to trauma and, in some cases, torture.

Furthermore, advocating for such newly arrived refugees can be challenging due to a number of factors, including the negative influence of media in regards to refugees and the expectations of refugees themselves upon arriving in Australia.

The challenges upon arrival

When refugees are coming to Australia, they focus all their energies on arriving safely. They want a safe and secure place for their family. When you ask refugees why they have come to Australia, their response is always the same: they came to Australia seeking a better life for their families. However, when they arrive here, they face the harsh reality of everyday life in a completely different and sometimes hostile environment.

Even though Australia offers a secure place for refugees to live, they face a number of challenges, which disrupt their previous way of living. In the current cohort of newly arrived refugees, there are a large number of single women who have come on a Woman in Risk Visa. There are also a large number of refugees who are illiterate in their own language, so learning English becomes a challenging priority for most of them. Further, the inability to speak English creates a barrier to finding employment, which leads to reliance on Government Centrelink benefits. In many cases, this support is not sufficient to cover their financial needs.

Navigating complex and inflexible bureaucratic systems in Australian can be overwhelming. There are guidelines and policies with which to comply. The system is black and white, where boxes need to be ticked regardless of individual personal circumstances. There are no exemptions for refugees. For example, mature-age women with very limited English are required to comply with job-active requirements regardless of their limitations, which causes stress.

Significantly, there are newly arrived refugees with complex needs. These reflect, in some instances, families coming from refugee camps where they lacked access to healthcare; often they require immediate access to healthcare upon arrival. However, they have to join the long waiting list and an already stretched healthcare system. This can lead to health conditions worsening through lack of treatment and sometimes they just give up.

Take the example of a woman refugee suffering from cataracts. With help from one of CatholicCare Melbourne's volunteers, she was able to get an appointment with a specialist who referred her to a hospital for an operation. A month later she received a letter advising that she had been placed on the waiting list with up to two years to wait for the operation. The woman's vision was getting worse daily, causing her distress in her everyday life. One day while carrying her child, she fell on the street. CatholicCare started advocating on her behalf, soon receiving an offer from a doctor to perform the operation at no cost to the patient. Needing financial support to cover the hospital fees, CatholicCare spoke with the local St Vincent de Paul Society conference, which graciously offered to pay the hospital fees. The operation was a success and the woman was beyond grateful for all the support received.

The challenges of settlement

Unrealistic expectations of life in Australia cause great challenges for newly arrived refugees in regards to what they thought they had been promised versus what they encounter. Refugee families struggle to secure sustainable and affordable housing. Obtaining a rental property in the private market is extremely difficult; they are required to attend open inspections and, if they do not drive a car, new problems arise. They then prefer to rent close to public transport where properties are more expensive.

Renting a house is a daunting process. Refugees are required to lodge an application, as are others. But, not having a rental history disadvantages them in comparison to other applicants who can demonstrate that they have the means to pay the rent, and a history of doing so. This leads to refugees wanting to obtain public housing, which is also attractive because of the hope it offers of an affordable long-term property from which they will not be required to move as they might have to in private rental.

However, the waiting list in the Department of Housing is extremely long. In many cases refugees ask CatholicCare to support them to complete an application for emergency housing. This process is more complicated because they have to comply with a series of requirements to be eligible. Often the waiting period is between 3-5 years.

Advocating for refugees, in a space where there is a lot of misinformation and myths about the real reason behind peoples' needs to migrate, is a challenge in the current political sphere. Media and propaganda influence the wider community. Linking Muslims with terrorism creates misinformation and diverts people from the real refugee journey and their stories, creating fear and intolerance. Refugee women often fear to go out because they are abused in public spaces, creating racial hostility.

Family challenges

Parenting in a new culture is not only different but also challenging. Parents arriving in a new country are struggling with their own problems in regards to lack of employment, inability to speak English, inadequate housing etc. These problems mean that often parents cannot pay full attention to their children's individual needs, creating conflicts in the families. Further, mothers and fathers sometimes have differences in parenting styles, ultimately affecting the children.

Another issue faced by newly arrived families is the way they discipline their children. Differences of practice have led to instances where families have been reported to child protection authorities and children have been removed from their parents' care and placed in the care of families in the community, adding more distress to the families.

Newly arrived families do not know much about the Australian education system. Their lack of knowledge combined with their lack of English creates an enormous barrier for them in communicating with the school and asking for assistance. There are also cases where children suffer the loss of those who were left behind which may affect their learning. Further, many young people are placed in high schools according to their age with no regard to previous education.

The challenges of the legal system

Newly arrived families have increasingly come into conflict with the law because of their ignorance of the law. For example, they learn to drive but sometimes ignore the road rules and are fined. The same happens with the use of myki cards for travel on public transport. Often people get fines for forgetting to activate the card and, as a result, end up with heavy fines. If people are given the option to go to court, they panic and prefer to pay the fine to avoid going to court. Understandably, as the majority of refugees have had bad experiences in dealing with police and the courts in their country of origin.

The CatholicCare Refugee and Settlement Program

There is an increasing requirement for proper settlement support to respond to newly arrived families' needs. Services have to be creative in engaging families with education programs to address their settlement needs and give them an understanding of the law.

The CatholicCare Refugee and Settlement Program works with newly arrived refugee and humanitarian entrants who have been in Australia up to five years.

The program provides culturally sensitive support to individuals and families to enhance their successful settlement in Australia. We work in collaboration and partnership with other service providers, local government and community-based organisations with the aim of achieving smooth transition towards permanent settlement. Our support groups provide a safe space for our participants, allowing them to learn English but also to make friends and address their isolation issues. Our groups and information sessions are facilitated by volunteers; some of our groups include the Afghan Women's Beginner English Conversation Group, Multicultural Men's English Conversation Group, Multicultural Women's Advanced English Conversation Group and the Multicultural Women's Sewing Program.

CatholicCare also runs justice education programs in partnership with the Dandenong Magistrates' Court. These consist of seven sessions when mainstream agencies, government departments and the police meet with a group of newly arrived refugees in a court room and present a topic of interest. Refugees have the opportunity to learn first-hand about the security process to access a court, and thereby are assisted to overcome their own fear of going to court. After doing this program they feel more relaxed, knowing that the court system is here to support the community not to punish them in the way many have experienced in their country. Magistrates, lawyers, sheriffs, police prosecutors and child protection officers are amongst the presenters. Participants have the opportunity to ask questions and present their own cases so advice can be provided.

Critical importance of advocacy

Difficult as it is in the current political atmosphere, it is very important to raise awareness of the real reasons behind refugees having to leave their homeland to seek a safe place to protect themselves and their family. This can be most effectively done from the grass roots level, where practitioners are experiencing the human face of refugees, dealing on a daily basis with real people and their struggles.

Advocacy is such a powerful tool. It is important to lobby at the government and policy level.

We also need to raise general awareness of the refugee reality and challenge many more members of our fortunate society to support them in their resettlement. We need eye specialists, lawyers, landlords, real estate agents etc. and employers in general who are able to lend a hand to refugees and assist their pursuit of a better life in their new country.

And this advocacy and awareness raising needs to be done in a way that supports the cause without imposing on and disempowering those in need.

CatholicCare and its partners strive to address these issues and empower, educate and support refugees to create a better life, negotiate through bureaucratic systems and settle into living in Australia. In line with the Church's commitment to social ministry, the services we provide are of high quality and tailored to meet individual needs and most importantly family needs.

Learning from the NDIS Pilot: The Experience of CatholicCare Canberra & Goulburn

Anne Kirwan with Helen Burt

The National Disability Insurance Scheme[105] (NDIS) is a nation-wide program initiated by the Federal Government to meet the support needs of people with a disability. The NDIS poses significant challenges for disability service providers in that it creates an open marketplace for service provision. It also places decision-making in the hands of the person receiving the services. Their supports are personalised to their individual needs, and they hold the funds and choose which organisation will provide the services and supports they require.

The NDIS commenced in trial sites prior to its full rollout across Australia. The Australian Capital Territory (ACT) was such a site, and the pilot there commenced in July 2014. CatholicCare Canberra & Goulburn (CatholicCare) is a disability support provider and participated in the pilot.

This chapter, which builds on a workshop delivered at the February 2016 Catholic Social Services conference,[106] provides insights into how CatholicCare responded to the challenge of the NDIS, from a viewpoint of 18 months into the pilot phase. It reflects that CatholicCare has worked on the principle that the main reasons people would choose it to provide their support under the NDIS are its staff, its mission and its values.

---

[105] For information on the NDIS, see www.ndis.gov.au, accessed on 17 June 2016.
[106] The February 2016 Catholic Social Services conference, *Review, Re-imagine, Renew: Mission making a difference in a changing world*, which inspired this volume, was held in Melbourne on 24-26 February 2016.

About CatholicCare Canberra & Goulburn

CatholicCare is the social services arm of the Archdiocese of Canberra and Goulburn and operates in the ACT and south-eastern New South Wales. The mission of CatholicCare is to uphold the dignity of each person by:

- providing high quality accessible services,
- empowering individuals, couples and families,
- promoting healthy, inclusive communities through relationships and collaboration for the common good.[107]

It is a substantial organisation with a $16 million annual turnover in social services, including approximately $8 million in disability and mental health services. Some 10,000 individuals and families receive services each year and, at the time of the conference workshop, the organisation had 270 staff.

Participating in the NDIS pilot

As a provider of services in the disability and mental health space, the rollout of the NDIS presented CatholicCare with a significant challenge. The NDIS required a different model of operation and focus, one that worked across all organisational areas including direct service provision, business services, marketing and community relations.

CatholicCare wished to continue providing disability and mental health services, so chose to become a provider of NDIS-funded services. This meant, however, that the organisation had to go through a significant change process. To underpin this change without losing its organisational mission and values CatholicCare needed to answer the questions:

- What is our core business?, and
- What is the role of Catholic social services in the lives of marginalised people?

---

[107] For information about CatholicCare Canberra & Goulburn, see www.catholiccare.cg.org.au; accessed on 16 June 2016.

The CatholicCare values of respect for the dignity of the human person, solidarity and stewardship fitted with the goals of the NDIS and the person-centred services that the NDIS sought to create.

The organisation believed that there was a place for it in the new market created by the NDIS. It wished to retain a current ministry and to attract new people and families to CatholicCare. The organisation concluded: "We are a quality provider, have a good reputation, and believe we provide a good service". Thus, through a process of discernment, CatholicCare chose to continue in this area of ministry.

Significantly, CatholicCare was going to face a challenging future, whether it participated in the NDIS or chose not to be part of it. If the organisation chose not to participate in the new market created by the NDIS, it would lose $8 million of disability and mental health services funding. This meant that 50 percent of its annual organisational income would transfer to packages and support through the NDIS provided by other organisations. CatholicCare's main focus, however, was its commitment to maintaining disability services as a key ministry.

Aware of this enormous challenge, CatholicCare commenced a dialogue about what this change would mean. What were the implications of NDIS? What service models, roles and positions would change? This required listening to and talking with each part of the organisation, to every department, program and person, about how NDIS would impact on them. CatholicCare did this relentlessly and at every opportunity.

Importantly, CatholicCare sent out a very positive and clear message, namely that CatholicCare as an organisation supported the NDIS. Without that, the change process risked being undermined. Creating a sense of negativity about the change could have made staff feel passive and 'stuck'.

CatholicCare found that the biggest internal challenge was not one that was faced by the direct care disability staff. They were all aware of the development of the NDIS and had known about self-directed funding for many years. It was staff in the other areas of the organisation, in housing and mental health services and the business sides of the organisation, who found the change more challenging. They found it difficult to understand the rationale for the changes and why they affected them when the changes were predominantly about the disability area. 'Buy-in' from these staff was critically important but more difficult.

CatholicCare made a considerable investment of time in managing the change process and managing staff through the changes. It invested in its staff and gave priority to caring for them. There was anxiety among the Board, the leadership team and many staff. What would happen to them? What would happen to the job they loved? What would happen to the agency and their clients?

Under the new NDIS model, some existing roles would not be required, and CatholicCare was therefore unable to give a guarantee to everyone that they would still have a job. This was particularly difficult because at the time when staff needed to be performing at their best, they were experiencing stress and uncertainty.

Resources were dedicated to strategic planning and research-based learning and, as part of this, a dedicated NDIS planning role was established. This person undertook all NDIS-related tasks and made sure that CatholicCare was aware of all the documents and policies that were being released by the National Disability Insurance Agency (NDIA), the agency running the NDIS.

All roles and structures in the organisation were reviewed and budget forecasts were developed. It was only then that the very difficult process of restructuring and rolling out targeted redundancies and role changes was begun.

Business planning and strategy required a great deal of research. Research indicated that CatholicCare could expect that 85 percent of clients would stay with its service, thus initially estimating around a 20 percent turnover. Being only an estimate, it was very difficult for CatholicCare's finance area to develop budgets based on this projection. As it turned out the estimation was wrong, and CatholicCare experienced only a one percent loss of existing clients.

A decision was made not to focus on significant growth during the first year of the trial, but to concentrate on maintaining high standards of service to clients. CatholicCare believed that to focus on growth in the first year of the trial would have too many risks associated with it. The organisation would have to make decisions to increase resources and make capital investments in an immature market when the future was unknown. Failure to meet growth targets had the potential to affect the long-term sustainability of CatholicCare. Therefore the main focus was on retaining existing clients and relationship building, thereby reinforcing the foundations of the organisation. Nevertheless, there was a 25 percent increase in the number of clients over the initial 18 months of the pilot, notwithstanding that growth was not specifically targeted.

Launching a new brand

Marketing had not been a major focus for CatholicCare. It had never had a need to promote its disability services as there had always been a waiting list. However, it realised this approach would not be enough in the new competitive NDIS environment.

CatholicCare engaged an advertising firm and, in the first phase, developed a new brand called 'CatholicCare CHOICES' together with a dedicated website, and began marketing its services at every opportunity. It is now moving into a second phase of this initiative with a new marketing plan and working on brand awareness.

In the above-mentioned first phase, ongoing engagement with current and potential clients was the major focus. It was important to keep engaged with existing clients and for clients to understand the NDIS. CatholicCare staff compiled a summary for each client of the supports they could receive from CatholicCare. This told the client how much support CHOICES would be able to provide for them under the NDIS, if they chose to continue with CatholicCare. It also gave the client information about this support if they were considering other organisations.

CatholicCare also assisted clients to complete the NDIS planning workbook, with its focus on their goals and aspirations. This helped clients to think about what they wanted to achieve under a model where they could direct their own funding and choose their supports.

The reality of finance

Under the NDIS model, only face-to-face or direct work with the clients is funded. There is no funding for back-of-house tasks that may support the face-to-face work. It was important that staff understood how tasks they previously did would be classified, and for what tasks there would be no funding in the future.

This funding formula also had a major impact on the rest of the organisation. The operational overheads carried by CatholicCare were around 20 percent, a good standard compared to the ACT social services sector, which averaged between 15 to 25 percent. But the goal of the NDIA was for overheads to run at between nine and 15 percent. CatholicCare needed to find efficiencies urgently to balance a reduction in overheads while still being able to function effectively. This has been an ongoing process, mainly achieved through using technologies to reduce overheads.

Under the NDIS, organisations have to think in terms of unit costing: how much it costs to provide one hour of service. When CatholicCare began the process their hourly cost was $56. Over the first 18 months of the pilot CatholicCare was able to reduce this cost dramatically to $46. But the NDIA only funds $42.77 per hour, so CatholicCare still had the ongoing challenge of reducing its costs from $46 to $42.77 per hour.

Cash flow has also been a significant issue. In the past, funding payments were made three months in advance. Under the NDIS, payments are made three days in arrears. CatholicCare has had to rely on money from other areas of the business to maintain its cash flow.

The new environment

After 18 months of operating within the NDIS environment, CatholicCare has seen a number of changes including:
- a great increase in competitors in the market,
- an increase in merges and consortiums,
- an increase in advertising by competitors, requiring

redirection of funds into marketing,

- a 25 percent growth in services, but not necessarily in operating surplus,
- an increase in referrals from families because of the Catholic mission of the organisation, but a clear message from other families that they will not consider a Catholic organisation, regardless of ability or skills (this is an increasingly polarised market),
- the 'Catholic brand' being damaged by the current publicity about sexual abuse within the Church, and that is something that CatholicCare acknowledges but cannot change,
- initially, clients staying with their existing provider while they waited to see how the NDIS works and how the market moved. However, this has changed as the market has become more stable.

CatholicCare's recommendations

After 18 months of operating in the new NDIS environment, CatholicCare offers other organisations in a similar situation the following recommendations:

- develop a flexible strategic plan so your approach can be adjusted as circumstances change,
- integrate your business systems to avoid duplication,
- map the customer journey so it is easy for customers to navigate your system,
- consider mentoring and coaching for leadership, as there will likely be little room for middle management roles,
- know your costs and test new products against different service models before beginning to provide support,
- do your market research so you know where your customers are and what supports people need.

Mission in the context of the NDIS

Mission is everything in the context of the NDIS. The experience of CatholicCare shows that it is easy for an agency to get lost in the challenge of responding to the NDIS, and to lose sight of its core purpose. In the face of difficulties it is important to be able to answer the following questions: What are your priorities? How do you behave? Which opportunity do you choose when opportunities are presented? What is your core business?

When CatholicCare was losing positions, it continued to invest in mission and pastoral care, retaining the mission engagement position and commencing a pastoral care role to support staff and their families. CatholicCare considered staff to be its greatest asset and did everything to ensure they were cared for, while also ensuring that agency values were being lived through the work they did.

Investing in mission engagement and pastoral care was not an easy decision to make in an environment where CatholicCare was losing positions. It came down to being able to articulate:

- who we are,
- why we are here.

As CEO I am constantly asking the leadership team what makes us different from just being a quality social services provider? What makes us a quality Catholic social services provider? If there is a difference, what is it? It cannot be that most staff are Catholic as CatholicCare has a truly diverse secular workforce. It must be something else. It must be what they do and why they do it.

The advice offered by CatholicCare, in the context of the NDIS, is that it is important to keep mission at the heart of the organisation. Finding and retaining good staff is crucial to the mission and success of the organisation because it is staff who enact the mission.

How staff reflect Catholic Social Teaching becomes the point of difference for an organisation. CatholicCare made a priority of deepening staff understanding of Catholic Social Teaching so, at very least, they knew how Catholic Social Teaching relates to their own values, and the way in which they work with clients and families.

Benefits of mission in the NDIS environment

Through its journey with the NDIS pilot and with its focus on mission, CatholicCare has found that:

- a strong engagement with mission builds performance and productivity,
- mission generates pride in the organisation,
- mission builds brand awareness,
- mission increases staff retention and loyalty,
- the mission creates a point of difference for the organisation,
- the mission requires an investment in brand, in culture and in staff.

Challenges of mission in the NDIS

There are challenges for mission in the context of the NDIS. Mission engagement requires energy and resources. Yet this happens at a time when energy and resources are also required for other areas, particularly cutting costs and focusing on new service models.

The NDIS can challenge the culture of the organisation. Good people leave as their roles no longer exist, and an organisation can generally only afford to retain the most productive people. This challenges an organisation to know its priorities and values. It also means that mission discernment is critical when making business decisions.

The key question

In engaging with the NDIS model, the key question that organisations need to ask themselves is: "Why would a client choose us?" Organisations need to be able to articulate answers to this question, to their clients, staff and other stakeholders.

CatholicCare has worked on the principle that the main reasons people would choose it to provide their support under the NDIS are its staff, its mission and its values.

Care of Older People from the Margins: The Trauma-Informed Approach at Sacred Heart Mission

Stephen Schmidtke and Marija Dragic with Michael Yore

If you were to reimagine, as creatively as you could, aged care services that met the particular needs of the most vulnerable elderly in the community, they might well look like the formal aged care support options provided by Sacred Heart Mission in the Melbourne suburb of St Kilda.[108]

Supporting people experiencing homelessness, or at risk of homelessness, has been a core focus for Sacred Heart Mission since its foundation in 1982. Entering as fully as possible into the world of those who move in and out of homelessness, staff and volunteers at Sacred Heart Mission are unequivocally committed to discovering ever more innovative, creative and ultimately more effective ways of enhancing the lives and the prospects of people experiencing long-term homelessness and persistent disadvantage. The Trauma and Homelessness Initiative is one very significant, even ground-breaking example of this pursuit of ever more effective ways of providing support to those on the margins.

But first, some context is required if the link between trauma and homelessness and the Mission's formal aged care support options is to make sense, and this needs to include a brief tour of the different services provided by Sacred Heart Mission. Like a giant jigsaw, they all fit together to provide as holistic an approach as possible to supporting the most marginalised people. The Mission's Service Model promotes an integrated and consistent approach to service delivery across the organisation. Integration across programs ensures clients receive the same service response irrespective of their point of access, and that they

---

[108] For further information on Sacred Heart Mission, see www.sacredheartmission.org/; accessed on 5 June 2016.

are not required to repeat their stories if they access more than one of the Mission's programs.

Sacred Heart Mission: the beginning

In 1982 the parish priest of Sacred Heart, St Kilda, Fr Ernie Smith, began sharing meals in his house with the homeless men who regularly knocked on his door seeking a sandwich. It could have remained at that, simply isolated acts of charity by a compassionate parish priest. But this was a parish priest who realised that homelessness, and the myriad issues associated with it, was endemic in and around St Kilda. Something more structured and organised was required to confront a problem that would not disappear because of a few shared meals.

Gathering around him a small group of committed parishioners and later, a few employed staff, Fr Ernie set about preparing simple meals on a regular and organised basis for people experiencing homelessness in what is now the City of Port Phillip in Melbourne.

The dining hall at Sacred Heart Mission today provides meals twice daily to hundreds of people and has become, for so many, the doorway into a wide variety of other support services provided to those most in need. The dining hall was, and remains, far more than just a place to satisfy physical hunger with a meal. It is a place of warmth, welcome and genuine community-building from which confidence may grow in those who find a welcome there to seek out more support and assistance.

Sacred Heart Mission has always been, and remains, first and foremost, a welcoming community, building relationships of trust and respect. As well as this, the commitment to innovation, ensuring that the services remain truly responsive and effective to needs, is underpinned by the quest for a constant development of knowledge which will provide the evidence to address effectively deep, persistent disadvantage and social exclusion. This search for new knowledge and new evidence is allied to a tradition of creativity and ensures that the Mission does not lose sight of the importance of contributing to systemic change.

Sacred Heart Mission's services

The services provided by Sacred Heart Mission are grouped into three categories, *Engagement Hubs, Individualised Planned Support* and *Longer Term Support and Accommodation*. Varied though they are, the services in all three categories are interconnected, enabling the possibility of addressing the support needs of the whole person rather than focussing only on addressing a particular and specific issue or challenge.

Engagement Hubs

This service consists of two engagement hubs:

- **Women's House:** providing a safe and welcoming space for women seeking assistance for a range of needs from housing and legal support to parenting assistance, companionship and a free lunch.

- **Sacred Heart Central:** providing a meals program 365 days a year and providing 3,000 free breakfasts and 8,000 free nutritious lunches every month (or 132,000 meals every year).

Individualised Planned Support

Several services are offered under this program:

- **Case Management:** providing individual assistance with housing, mental health, legal and medical needs, and social and life skills.

- **Hands on Health Clinic:** a variety of complementary health and alternative therapies including massage, chiropractic, homeopathy, counselling, acupuncture, hairdressing and optometry.

- **Homefront:** short-term, crisis accommodation and intensive case management for single women over the age of 25 years.

- **Women, Housing and Complex Needs Program:** intensive, longer-term support and case coordination for women who are homeless or at risk of homelessness and who have multiple and complex needs.

- **Resource Room:** making available information and referrals for housing assistance, medical care, financial and specialist support services, as well as shower and laundry facilities.

- **Specialist Services Team:** case management for people with complex needs and behaviours, particularly mental health and drug-and-alcohol related issues.

- **Kick Start – Health and Wellbeing:** intensive support to assist people to develop healthier lives and independence through sport and other activities.

- **Outlandish:** opportunities for women to get involved in eco-volunteering and a service designed to support women who would benefit from increased community participation.

- **Pastoral Care:** offering a person-centred, holistic approach to care that complements the care offered by other disciplines whilst paying particular attention to spiritual care.

Longer-Term Support and Accommodation

The longer-term support services encompass the following:

- **Sacred Heart Community:** a mix of high and low care accommodation for 83 older people who have experienced homelessness or disadvantage during their lives.

- **Home Care:** support and care to people who have age-related conditions and live in the cities of Port Phillip, Glen Eira and Stonnington, assisting them to remain at home.

- **Rooming House Plus:** long-term, secure accommodation provided for 67 residents with a history of homelessness and complex needs.

- **Bethlehem Community:** a safe community-based living environment with medium- and long-term accommodation, outreach and support to women who are homeless.

It is to this third grouping of services, the provision of longer-term accommodation and its concomitant support services to which we now turn, with a special focus on the care of older people who have experienced homelessness and trauma. With the population of people experiencing homelessness rapidly growing older, as with the Australian population generally, the challenge is to provide aged care support and accommodation tailored specifically to the needs of people who have experienced entrenched social exclusion because of homelessness. The *Trauma and Homelessness Initiative* aims to do this by achieving better outcomes for people who are homeless and have experienced trauma.

Homelessness in Australia

The Australian Bureau of Statistics' 2011 Census[109] revealed more than 105,000 people experiencing homelessness in Australia on Census night, more people than an MCG crowd on Grand Final Day. This was an increase of eight percent from the previous Census. It has been estimated that around 21,000 of these people are the long-term homeless. Again, according to the Australian Bureau of Statistics, one in seven of those experiencing homelessness (14,851 people) were over the age of 55, although older people of this age are more likely than younger people who are homeless to be staying in boarding houses or other households.

Those experiencing homelessness who come into contact with one or more of the services provided by Sacred Heart Mission are likely, in significant numbers, to have experienced abuse and trauma; to have histories of serious mental health issues; to be financially very disadvantaged; and to be socially isolated and dislocated from community of any kind. Those assisted also include those people supported by the

---

[109] Australian Bureau of Statistics (ABS), 2012. *Census of Population and Housing: Estimating Homelessness, 2011*, Catalogue No. 2049.0. Canberra: ABS; accessed on 5 June 2016 at www.abs.gov.au.

Home Care program, which assists the mainly elderly population using the service to remain at home.

People who experience homelessness and trauma, deep and persistent disadvantage, and social isolation, do not readily access aged care services. This is partly because there are few aged care services that cater to the specific needs of this cohort, often because of assumptions made by the aged care sector itself and the population generally, and partly because of the assumptions and past experiences of the cohort themselves.

Against this background, Sacred Heart Mission, committed to looking continuously for more effective ways of caring for older people from the margins and determined to achieve the best outcomes for them, embarked upon researching the links between trauma and homelessness. Two significant pieces of research inform the Mission's work, namely the Journey to Social Inclusion and the Trauma and Homelessness Initiative.

The Journey to Social Inclusion (J2SI)

Launched in November 2009, J2SI was a three year pilot program that aimed to assist 40 people to make a permanent exit from long-term homelessness. It was a significant departure from existing approaches and set s a new benchmark for addressing long-term homelessness in Australia. It takes a relationship-based approach, provides long-term intensive support, and works from the premise that if people can sustain their housing and manage their complex health issues, this provides a solid foundation for the next steps of building skills, becoming a part of the community and contributing to society.

The J2SI pilot, which supported 40 people over three years, delivered impressive results. A study undertaken a year after service delivery came to an end, showed that 75 percent of participants remained in stable housing after four years, 80 percent had seen a decline in the need for health services[110] and the pilot offered savings to government of $29,864 per participant.[111] Ultimately J2SI works from a trauma-informed approach, it saves lives, reduces reliance on the service system including expensive health and emergency services, and prevents people from being incarcerated.

Sacred Heart Mission is currently undertaking the second phase of the program. Through partnerships with VincentCare (Ozanam Community Centre) and St Mary's House of Welcome, the Mission is supporting 60 people who have experienced long-term, chronic homelessness for up to three years.

The findings from J2SI research contribute to aged care services delivery and caring for older people from the margins across the Mission.

The Trauma and Homelessness Initiative

Sacred Heart Mission, in collaboration with three other organisations that provide homelessness and mental health services in the community, MIND Australia, Inner South Community Health and VincentCare Victoria,[112] established the Trauma and Homelessness Initiative[113] with the aim of achieving better outcomes for people who are long-term homeless and have experienced trauma.

The organisations commissioned Phoenix Australia,[114] formerly

---

[110] G. Johnson, D. Kuehnle, S. Parkinson, S. Sesa, & Y. Tseng (2014). *Sustaining exits from long-term homelessness: A randomised controlled trial examining the 48 month social outcomes from the Journey to Social Inclusion pilot program*. St. Kilda: Sacred Heart Mission, p. 4; accessed on 18 August 2016 at www.sacredheartmission.org/sites/default/files/publication-documents/j2si_sustaining_exits_from_longterm_homelessness_2015.pdf.

[111] Ibid., p. 25.

[112] For information on MIND Australia, Inner South Community Health and VincentCare Victoria, see respectively www.mindaustralia.org.au, ischs.org.au/ and vincentcare.org.au/; accessed on 5 June 2016.

[113] For further background on the Trauma and Homelessness Initiative, see www.sacredheartmission.org/understanding-homelessness/trauma-homelessness-initiative; accessed on 5 June 2016.

[114] For information on Phoenix Australia – Centre for Posttraumatic Mental Health, see www.phoenixaustralia.org; accessed on 5 June 2016.

known as the Australian Centre for Post-traumatic Mental Health (ACPMH) at the University of Melbourne, to look at the relationship of traumatic events in people's lives and their state of homelessness. The central focus of the initiative was on people who were either already experiencing long-term homelessness or were seriously at risk of becoming homeless. This group of people typically move in and out of homelessness or constantly live with the threat of homelessness, often moving between the street, institutions and poor quality temporary housing.

In the study carried out by ACPMH,[115] trauma could be a single traumatic event (Type 1 Trauma), such as a motor vehicle accident, or a series of complex, prolonged, interpersonal events, such as child abuse (Type 2 Trauma). The research aimed at addressing questions such as:

- What is the link between trauma and homelessness?
- What are typically the kinds of traumatic events experienced by people who have also experienced homelessness?
- Importantly, does the experience of trauma contribute to homelessness?
- What are the main mental health issues that accompany people experiencing, or at risk of, homelessness?
- What levels of social support and community connectedness are experienced by people who are homeless?
- What are the barriers to seeking help for issues related to trauma and mental health?

The research included an extensive literature review and two qualitative studies with staff of the four consortium organisations and with people being supported by these partner agencies. Finally, an in-depth survey interview of 115 randomly selected participants was undertaken, making this research project one of the largest ever in Australia to examine the relationship between trauma and homelessness.

---

[115] M. O'Donnell, T. Varker, R. Cash, R. Armstrong, L. Di Censo, P. Zanatta, A. Murnane, L. Brophy & A. Phelps (2014). *The Trauma and Homelessness Initiative*. Report prepared by the Australian Centre for Posttraumatic Mental Health in collaboration with Sacred Heart Mission, Mind Australia, Inner South Community Health and VincentCare Victoria; accessed on 18 August 2016 at www.sacredheartmission.org/sites/default/files/publication-documents/THI_Report_research%20findings.pdf.

The research findings

What the research discovered regarding the twin experiences of trauma and homelessness confirmed what experienced workers in both the areas of homelessness and mental health services had long believed, namely, that there is an insidious relationship between trauma and homelessness. The research found:

- An extremely high level of reported exposure to traumatic events with *all* 115 participants reporting at least one traumatic event in their lifetime. Type 1 trauma, the single incident, was experienced by 98 percent of participants.
- High levels of exposure to interpersonal violence, including sexual and physical assault or Type 2 trauma. Prolonged and repeated traumatic events had been experienced by 60 percent of the participants.
- Nearly all participants (97%) were exposed to more than four traumatic events in their lifetime. This is compared to an average four percent rate in the general population.
- Significantly, 70 percent of participants experienced at least one traumatic event before experiencing homelessness, the majority having been exposed to trauma during childhood.
- Trauma was identified by participants as precipitating homelessness and exposure to trauma also occurred after becoming homeless.
- The criteria for a current mental health problem, such as post-traumatic stress disorder, depression, substance abuse and dependence and so on, were met by 88 percent of participants.
- Participants reported high levels of those symptoms associated with prolonged exposure to traumatic events, such as difficulty maintaining social relationships, risk taking and suicide ideation.

What the study quite clearly shows is that:

- **Trauma drives homelessness:** traumatic events often occur as a precursor to becoming homeless. The research showed that many people left home to avoid continued trauma in the form of assault, child abuse and other forms of violence.

- **Homelessness drives trauma exposure:** being homeless unquestionably puts people in harm's way exposing them to the risk of further trauma.
- **Trauma drives social difficulties:** the experience of trauma has a serious impact on an individual's sense of safety, trust of others and connection to people, especially if the trauma was caused by a primary care-giver.
- **Trauma drives mental health problems:** exposure to traumatic events in both childhood and adulthood are associated with mental health problems. The research showed clearly that the prevalence of mental health disorders was high amongst this group.

Implications of the Trauma and Homelessness Initiative

There are numerous implications for training of staff and volunteers as well as for service delivery resulting from the Trauma and Homelessness Initiative.

Trauma awareness

Raising awareness of the connection between trauma and homelessness and grasping the findings of the research are key to designing and developing services that bring about better outcomes, especially for older people requiring support and aged care. Organisational training and development are imperative. All Sacred Heart staff, volunteers and Board Directors are being trained in trauma awareness practice in order to develop an understanding across the entire organisation of the impact of trauma upon the lives of those with whom the Mission works.

Promoting safety

In the context of trauma awareness, safety refers to basic needs such as the need for physical and emotional safety. It refers to having access to food, shelter, medical assistance and such things as adequate financial and material assistance. Promoting safety involves providing accurate information about how to access these resources as well as assisting people to manage their current and future environments so that they develop greater skills to handle safety issues and identify and reduce exposure to continuing threats of harm.

Rebuilding control

Improving those skills required for psychosocial stability is key to helping people recover from trauma. Staff are supported in their engagement with those using Sacred Heart Mission's services to incorporate the use of psychosocial stability skills that can be learned and strengthened so that they can make a significant and sustainable contribution to recovery from trauma. This is strongly linked to embedding strengths-based practice into working with people who have experienced trauma. It is important to communicate the powerful message that people can cope, recover and move beyond the effects of past difficult and traumatic experiences.

Promoting connection

An important aspect on the road to recovery from trauma is promoting connections between people who have experienced trauma and their family, friends and others who may be significant in their lives, including other services. Such connection may mean, for instance, helping the person to enhance the networks and relationships they have with important community resources, or reinforcing the imperative to seek help by attending to immediate needs and concerns promptly. Very importantly, relationships between service providers and service users are often central to recovery. These relationships are supported by being clear about roles, boundaries and limits and by respecting diversity.

Belief in recovery

Conveying the conviction that recovery is possible enables hope and self-belief in those who have experienced trauma. Staff do this by being non-judgmental, modelling tolerance and acceptance, and constantly encouraging and actively supporting a person's engagement with the goals and supports that will lead to recovery. Staff approach challenging behaviour as a person's best effort to solve problems and, by being available to work through the issues that interfere with a person being able to access the services they need, they assist in recovery in a very practical way.

A new service model

The aspects mentioned above provide some practical and concrete steps that reflect the major outcome of the Trauma and Homelessness Initiative for Sacred Heart Mission, namely the development and implementation of a *new service model* which ensures consistent and integrated processes right across the organisation, facilitating a seamless pathway for those who use the Mission's services.[116] Integration across all programs ensures that everyone receives the same service response irrespective of their point of entry and are thus not required to repeat their stories if they require more than one of the Mission's services. This development of a seamless and integrated pathway through services is facilitated in a number of crucial ways by:

- obtaining organisation-wide consent from those requesting a service, asking them if they receive other Mission services and explaining that information may be shared across program areas to ensure an integrated plan,
- developing a strong team approach within and across program areas with new systems for sharing information,
- establishing regular contact between key workers when someone is accessing multiple Sacred Heart Mission services. This is to ensure a consistent approach and, importantly, reduces duplication and 'over servicing'. It may also result in a formal Shared Response Plan,
- educating key workers in different program areas to focus strongly on facilitating integration, for example, between the Assistance with Care and Housing for the Aged role and the

---

[116] For more information, see www.sacredheartmission.org/understanding-homelessness/homelessness-projects-reports; accessed on 10 July 2016.

Mental Health Case Worker, and

- implementation of an integrated outcomes measurement framework which has clear protocols for consistent data collection and reporting right across all program areas.

Sacred Heart Mission is presently creating a tool to measure the impact of the first year of this important initiative which is changing training and practice development across the organisation.

To reimagine the shape of services for older people so that they are truly life-enhancing for those who have experienced trauma and homelessness requires innovation and creativity. But that creativity must rest on the solid foundation of research such as the Trauma and Homelessness Initiative.

Like Sacred Heart Mission, other organisations might reflect on what some of the barriers are that people from the margins experience in accessing their services, and what they could do to address these by a completely different and innovative response.

More than Giving Back: Maximising the Mission Impact of Volunteers

Lisa McDonald

Beautiful Roma

Roma was one of those special people whom everyone loved, despite being a fanatical football fan. She had other redeeming qualities such as being a clever card player, a devoted mum and nana, and a happy presence to the socially vulnerable people, the friends, who had come to rely upon their daily visit to Briar Terrace, a place where they knew they would be welcomed and cherished.[117] When Roma died suddenly, we were all at a loss. The funeral of our beloved volunteer was attended by many of us from St Vincent's Hospital Melbourne, though most notably by many of the friends of Briar Terrace whom Roma had greeted at the door each day with a warm smile, a cup of coffee and a laugh. She made a difference in their lives and, by choosing to enhance one of our hospital services through the gift of her time, she made a difference in ours.

Significantly, Roma was a volunteer. She filled the role very capably in terms of the tasks that were required, offering companionship, hospitality, catering, occasional cleaning and supervision on outings. However, she volunteered much more than that, she volunteered her *self*, the unique aspects of character, personal qualities and temperament that are God-given and are offered discretionally, only.

> You may be able to 'buy' a person's back with a paycheck, position, power or fear but a human being's genius, loyalty and tenacious creativity are volunteered only. The world's greatest problems will be solved by passionate, unleashed 'volunteers'.[118]

---

[117] Part of St Vincent's Hospital Melbourne, Briar Terrace is a small cottage on Fitzroy Street, Fitzroy which supports locals who are experiencing social isolation.
[118] S.R. Covey, 2012. Foreword in L. D. Marquet, *Turn The Ship Around!: How to Create Leadership at Every Level*. Austin, Texas: Greenleaf Book Group Press.

Rich, diverse and multi-layered

The mission impact of volunteers is not singular; it is rich, diverse and multi-layered. Roma, through her example, helped us at St Vincent's Hospital to see the full extent of this:

1. Volunteers contribute in a special way to our mission through the roles they fulfil in our organisation.

2. Mission is impacted to an even greater extent when a volunteer brings their passion, their heartfelt effort and their unique personhood to their work.

3. A third and exceptional level of impact to be observed is when volunteers 'volunteer' their heart and soul through discretionary effort and by doing so model for staff a new way in which we might go about our daily work. Instead of looking at our work as a daily chore or a series of meetings, as staff we too can gift our organisation by also volunteering our genius, our loyalty and our tenacious creativity.

Pope Benedict XVI knew this to be true when he offered the following thought in his encyclical, *God is Love*:

> Those who work for the Church's charitable organisations must be distinguished by the fact that they do not merely meet the needs of the moment, but they dedicate themselves to others with heartfelt concern, enabling them to experience the richness of their humanity. Consequently, in addition to their professional training … they need to be led to that encounter with God in Christ which awakens their love and opens their spirits to others. As a result, love thy neighbour will no longer be for them a commandment imposed, so to speak, from without, but a consequence deriving from their faith, a faith which becomes active through love.[119]

When faith becomes active through love, volunteers and staff form a community of people who have a mission impact far beyond hours served. They have an impact upon the future of the whole organisation and, by doing so, reveal something of the light of Christ.

---

[119] Pope Benedict XVI, 2005. Encyclical Letter: *Deus Caritas Est*. Vatican City: Vatican, Section 31; accessed on 5 April 2016 at w2.vatican.va.

This is personal

We know that people choose to volunteer for a variety of reasons. Some are looking to fill their days meaningfully, others are looking to build their confidence for a little while before re-entering the workforce, some seek to widen their friendship circle, others have been put on the roster by their husband/wife/friend/son/daughter. Many feel passionately about an organisation's vision and mission. One honest fellow told us that the hospital was on his bus route, to which we replied, "That may be why you have come, but there will be many more reasons why you will stay".

With some considered exceptions, we usually take them all. It is wise to hold a worldview that sees everyone as having something to give, no matter why it is they have come. We have learned that we just have to be creative about finding the best spot for each person. Another reason for holding this worldview is because a diverse volunteer population is most effective when an organisation is trying to reach an equally diverse client, patient or community demographic. We are delighted to have within our ranks volunteers of many cultural backgrounds, ages and life stages.

It can be difficult to attract the numbers of volunteers that a service may have attracted thirty years ago. Increasing economic pressure has meant that people who would have previously had the time to allocate to volunteer activities, need to work longer than they might have expected and are less available during the day. Volunteer service managers are now becoming quite adept at adapting the responsibilities to suit the time people have available to come, where this was not always the case.

Yet, it is inspiring, even in these circumstances, that people still choose to go out of their way to assist and to offer their precious time so freely. We have tremendous hope for the future when we see younger generations volunteer through the social justice or community service arm of their school. In addition, some come in their own time after school. There is a renewed focus in education to understand social justice and to seek the development of the whole person, including their sense of citizenship and service. Through this momentum we have the opportunity not only to benefit in relation to direct provision of our services, but also to contribute to forming young people to be socially responsible, so that in our old age they will create and lead compassionate societies and just structures to look after us.

At the hospital we have found that a number of volunteers are motivated to join us because of their connection with our place; a family member or a friend was treated for their illness or may have died here. Our hospital has special meaning for them and they are here to give back. But what happens is more than giving back. The volunteers, through their generosity and service, become a part of our healing ministry and a part of our story. Our hospital, which holds a special place in their life, continues to play a role in their own journey through grief and recovery, healing and hope. From sadness, life is sourced again and the compassion they bring to their daily activities shines through to the patients.

It is not only in the healing ministries where this quality can be found. Think of people who have volunteered for a football club for many years and who rally around a family, a player or each other when a tragedy strikes.

Volunteering has a way of affirming humanity, which God so loves.

There are many gifts

> Now there are varieties of gifts, but the same Spirit. And there are varieties of services, but the same Lord; and there are varieties of activities, but it is the same God who activates all of them in everyone. To each is given the manifestation of the spirit for the common good. (1 *Corinthians* 12:4-7)

My husband is an Anglican minister. Occasionally I have come across the quiet hopes of his parishioners about things that they think I will volunteer to do, as the minister's wife. On one occasion, Mark looked very sheepish when telling me about a group who had approached him to suggest that I run the kitchen at the church camp. Filled with terror, I asked him, "What did you say?" He told me very proudly, "Don't worry. I let them know in no uncertain terms that you'd be quite incompetent doing that, that they should really look for someone else to do the job". Thank heavens! My relief was instant. I am a terrible cook; the group would have starved. "Yes, but did you also tell them that I'd be happy to help in other ways, such as emceeing the concert, or pastoral care? Those are things I love to do and I really do have a servant's heart!", I offered.

"Oh yes, I probably should have mentioned that …", he said, slinking away into the distance.

As all good volunteer managers know, there is an art to matching the right role to the person and people really do arrive at your doorstep with all of their quirky loveliness, which absolutely must be appreciated and taken into account. It is not always easy to get it right the first time but, with experience and flexibility, some wonderful decisions can be made that bring life to the volunteer and the situation. Taking the opportunity in the initial volunteer interview to get to know the person, to ask them about their reasons for volunteering and what they hope to achieve through volunteering, and exploring some of the options available are key strategies in volunteer management which are useful at this stage. Trusting your intuition is equally as useful.

The St Vincent's Hospital volunteer pet therapy program requires a person with the right combination of care, command (with animals) and the ability to read the situation to ensure the experience is only ever positive for the patient. Our administration volunteers need to be happy to work on their own for the best part of a day. Our Angel Program volunteers need to be flexible with time, prepared to undergo training and good at assisting a person in need. There are times when volunteering unexpectedly shines a light on a gift or talent the person did not previously know they had. There are times when volunteering shines a light on a need the organisation did not previously realise that it had.

There is a simple definition of ministry that describes it as "the intersection between gift and need". In our places of work, especially in a hospital, the need is very well established. When volunteers generously offer the gifts they have been given by the Spirit, these meet the need and the impact is a blessing which enables the continuation of our mission.

Down to business

- "We are not a Hospital with a mission. We are a Mission with a hospital".
- The mission comes first, it precedes the organisation which

came about in order to fulfil it.

- Mission is our business and our business is a ministry.

Organisations of every kind spend a lot of time and often money on business development and on developing a strategic plan. Ours is a ten-year plan and in it we are implored to serve, see and strive for something greater.[120] The goals are aspirational but are also reflective of the organisation's *raison d'etre*, our reason for being. Staff are introduced to our strategic plan during their orientation at St Vincent's. It is important that they know our vision and how we plan to get there so they may contribute to it.

Our volunteers all attend our normal hospital orientation program. We do this because they are a key part of how we hope to achieve the plan. Furthermore, it inspires them and energises them further. They come to a fuller appreciation of the context of the role that they play in its wider context and they too can take pride in our collective achievements as they occur.

In our experience, volunteers have invigorated key projects and we have discovered they are knowledgeable and pro-active stakeholders with insights to share. We have been wise to listen to them in recent years, particularly in such forums as our Community Advisory Committee where people who have experienced our care contribute to quality improvement activities of our hospital service.

We have recently embarked on a project affectionately known as 'Blue Coats', a concierge type service at the key entry points of our large campus in Fitzroy. We initiated a trial week and asked volunteers to compile data and feedback for us. At the end of the week we gathered for a meeting to collect all of this valuable information and we were astounded with how precise and useful it was. We have since designed the program based entirely on their feedback and volunteers have also offered their time to staff it on an ongoing basis, which is an extraordinary contribution.

---

[120] St Vincent's Health Australia (SVHA), 2015. *enVision 2025*. Sydney: SVHA; accessed on 8 April at svha.org.au/home/about-us/our-strategy-2025.

Inspired by grace

Our volunteer manager called one day to share the encounter that one of our volunteers had with a patient. An asylum seeker had been in our hospital for a long period of time and staff, including psychiatrists, pastoral carers, nurses and allied health practitioners, had been struggling to lift her mood for many weeks. Our volunteer, trained, ready and able, went to the ward with Bertie, a pooch from our volunteer pet therapy program. Our patient's mood lifted instantly upon seeing Bertie and she was transformed, even for a few moments, out of the midst of heavy gloom.

An inspired gentleman by the name of Tony Neylan volunteered many years of his life to nurturing Catholic young adult communities across Sydney and Australia, such was his belief in them and his calling and gifting from God. Though he knew and lived the Gospel intimately, he had a neat way of describing it, in a nutshell:

We are Loved

We are Forgiven

We are Healed

We are Called

We are Filled with the Spirit

We are Sent forth.

Each of these is present in the work of volunteers in our communities and organisations and across the world. Volunteers are Gospel bearers, the deliverers of good news, and mission is certainly accomplished when they infuse each encounter with nothing less than the exquisite feeling of being cared for, by another, by the 'universe', by God.

Conclusion

Denis Fitzgerald

The driving forces behind the conference *Review, Reimagine, Renew: Mission making a difference in a changing world* included the rapidly evolving environment in which we operate and the need to engage deeply with our mission to ensure that our response to change is mission-driven. In particular, we are impacted upon by changes in society, in programs and funding, and in the Church.

The chapters of this book have captured much of the content of specific conference sessions: examinations of mission and its implications for our activities and our organisations, various challenges arising within society and within the Church, and a number of areas of vulnerability and need where we are challenged to respond in a new or different way.

But there was so much more than has been able to be captured between these pages. A successful conference is greater than the sum of its parts. Ways in which *Review, Reimagine, Renew* advanced its purposes other than through the transmission of specific content included:
- the conference narrative: challenging, open, interactive,
- the participation of appropriate people and organisations,
- focusing on the right ideas,
- integrating the spiritual,
- an invitation to continue the journey.

The conference narrative: challenging, open, interactive

Over the course of three days, participants were invited to engage with the ideas presented and with the people around them.

Important pre-conditions for this engagement were bringing people together around a theme, and allowing time and space for interaction.

The latter was designed into the program: generous breaks and space in which to mix; and provision in almost all sessions for extensive interaction with participants.

The opening forum on the Church and family violence (see pp. 83-95) set the tone. The panel members provided varying perspectives on the deep roots in our culture that underpin violence against women; discussion was robust, with challenging issues, such as gender equality within the Church being well-aired, and Bishop Vincent Long OFMConv boldly responding on an issue where Church leaders in Australia have not been very prominent.

This tone of challenge, openness and interactivity continued through to the closing session of the conference, Professor Frank Brennan SJ's masterclass on Catholic Social Teaching (see pp. 47-60). Fr Frank's method was to outline an approach to the application of Catholic Social Teaching by means of a contemporary issue, and to invite discussion and comment, which were readily forthcoming.

The nature of some of the sessions determined the extent to which the floor could be thrown open. For example, Tony Nicholson's workshop topic of 'Money or Mission' (see pp. 115-124) was one where there was much to share around the room, whereas the workshop led by Tomasa Morales and Deacon George Peach Meat (for Tomasa's paper, see pp. 159-164) was more in the nature of an invitation to enter into the experience of these two session leaders. But in all cases appropriate challenge, openness and interaction were prominent.

The participation of appropriate people and organisations

Ultimately, ideas move and grow between people. As René Bouwen put it, "Knowledge is not something between the ears, it's something between the noses".[121] So, you need the right people. In a Catholic social services setting, this also requires the involvement of the right organisations.

---

[121] Quoted at p. 45 in C. Hoodendijk, 2015. *Appreciative Enquires of the 3.0 Kind;* accessed on 11 July 2016 at www.dropbox.com/s/yr8c5uxuwy5bqsa/Appreciative%20Inquiries%20of%20the%203.0%20Kind%20-%20Cees%20Hoogendijk.pdf?dl=0.

Leaders of Catholic social services from across the country participated: Board members and staff from Catholic Social Services Victoria and Catholic Social Services Australia, senior executives from nearly all States and Territories, and a range of Board members, practitioners, mission leaders, members of auspicing bodies, etc.

This was a rich mix that brought practical experience as well as informed reflection to bear throughout the conference. It included inspirational leaders, emerging leaders and, from some organisations, groups of people who were able to take a shared experience back to their own environment.

There was a focus on attracting future leaders and including smaller organisations, people who often are not able to attend such gatherings. Sponsorship was a great help here, as it removed part of any financial barrier to participation.

Church leaders, including Bishop Vincent Long OFMConv and Bishop Mark Edwards OMI, were a welcome presence. In addition to their substantive contributions to discussion (see, for example, Bishop Vincent's reflections on family violence, pp. 93-95), their presence reinforced to others their understanding of the importance of this sector for the Church as a whole.

A selection of leaders from outside our sector added to our considerations. Paul Linossier from Wesley Mission, Deb Tsorbaris from the Centre for Excellence in Child and Family Welfare, Robert Fitzgerald AM from the Royal Commission into Institutional Responses to Child Sexual Abuse and Tony Nicholson from the Brotherhood of St Laurence were among the high profile participants who ensured that discussion was not too inward looking, and that we took a realistic perspective on Catholic social services and other ministries. Similarly, leaders from other areas of Catholic endeavour, such as health, education, parishes and other ministries, broadened discussion and provided enriching insights.

Focusing on the right ideas

As the chapters of this book illustrate, the conference was seeded with topics that spoke to the heart of the dominant theme: *Mission making a difference in a changing world.*

Authentic engagement with this theme could not avoid the shadow and challenge of child sexual abuse and the Church's response to it. The presence and impact of Pope Francis, our awakening to the extent of family violence in our society, the pressures on our organisations from Governments and the markets they are creating: these too are part of most conversations on mission and change.

These topics were on the program. They were not new to participants, but the program focus raised levels of knowledge and awareness, and fed into the broader discussions that spilled over into corridors and coffee breaks. They formed part of the background against which other matters were considered.

There were other topics presented that have not featured in this book: Simon Habel from Catholic Earthcare Australia led a workshop on Pope Francis' encyclical on the environment; Vicki Clark's workshop provided an introduction to Aboriginal ceremony and its relevance to a modern spiritual community; the imperative to extend the role of women in the Church emerged as a theme in several plenary discussions; etc. These themes emerged from pre-conference discernment, and responded to nascent interest among participants.

Engaging with Indigenous Australia was also woven into the fabric of conference proceedings. Charlie King, a Gurindji man and prominent leader from the Northern Territory, contributed to the opening forum on family violence, and the conference officially began with a Welcome to Country by Wurundjeri Elder Colin Hunter.

At the official opening we also welcomed our Catholic Social Services Victoria message stick, a gift from Aboriginal Catholic Ministry Melbourne, which remained prominently placed with other symbols throughout the conference. They reminded us that we are united in faith and respect with our Aboriginal sisters and brothers and with each other from near and far, even as the themes of acknowledgement and of obligation to closing the gap emerged through the various conference sessions. These symbols were removed at the end of the conference, to the words of poet Betty Pike's 'An Australian Blessing':

> May you always stand tall as a tree
>
> Be as strong as the rock Uluru
>
> As gentle and still as the morning mist
>
> Hold the warmth of the campfire in your heart
>
> And may the Creator Spirit always walk with you.[122]

Integrating the spiritual

Catholic social services are a response to the Gospel calling to love of neighbour, and thus part of the mission of the Church. As discussed in the 'Introduction', involvement in these services is a spiritual undertaking, and a focus of the conference was on exploration of our mission.

Prayer, reflection and liturgy therefore had a vital role to play.

A simple, modelling element of prayer and ritual was built into the structure of the conference, and its documentation. There was an opening and a closing liturgy (each with Indigenous themes), a conference Mass, and music and reflections as gathering points during the conference. Vicki Clark, formerly of Aboriginal Catholic Ministry Melbourne, commented: "I loved the calling of people back into the main auditorium with … singing; it reminded me of the ancient, spiritual ground-to-earth culture way of bringing people together. Well done!"

And there was a conference prayer: *A Call to Mission – Making a Difference*:

> God of mercy, you call each of us to your mission
> of love and compassion in our world.
> As we review our story give us discerning spirits,
> and the humility to learn from our actions and missed opportunities

---

[122] E. Pike, 2011. *The Power of Story: Spirit of the Dreaming*. Mulgrave: John Garratt Publishing.

> Inspire us to reimagine in ourselves a greater creativity and courage
> to respond wholeheartedly to a changing world.
> Renew in us a passion for your mission of justice, mercy and
> service, especially towards those most marginalised.
> Strengthen our commitment to the common good,
> in the spirit of St Mary MacKillop
> who made a life-giving difference to so many.
> We make this prayer in Jesus' name.
> Amen.

The underlying idea was to integrate the spiritual into the fabric of the gathering, to inform our work, and to model an approach to the sacred that participants could take back to their services with them. It was well received.

An invitation to continue the journey

Our closing ceremony was a simple affair with three delegates sharing their memorable impressions or moments of the conference followed by the reading of Betty Pike's Australian blessing and a song as the message stick preceded the delegates out of the main hall to the dining room for our final meal together. Delegates were enlivened and encouraged to continue their re-imagining and the renewing of commitment to Gospel-inspired justice and action in their various communities of engagement.

But that was, in a sense, only the beginning. The task remains for participants and their organisations to respond to the rapidly changing environment in which mission must operate; and the hope is that participation in the conference better equipped them to do this.

This book is another contribution to the same end. It makes available to a wider group much of the material presented at the conference, and it invites readers to join in the engagement with our Christian mission of service and work for justice. And for those who did participate in the conference, the chapters are presented as an *aide memoire*, to nurture the reflection and call to action with which the various presenters and writers challenge us.

Catholic Social Services Victoria, the 2016 conference initiator, continues its dialogue with member organisations on mission and identity, as does Catholic Social Services Australia and each of the other organisations that participated. This book should enrich these various initiatives, and serve as a building block for deeper and more robust dialogue, and for a stronger and richer contribution to the wellbeing of individuals and communities on the margins of Australian society.

Contributors

John Allen Jnr

John L. Allen Jnr is the editor of *Crux*, an independent Catholic news site presented in partnership with the Knights of Columbus, and previously served both as a senior correspondent for the *National Catholic Reporter* and later as associate editor of the *Boston Globe*. He is the senior Vatican analyst for CNN, the author of ten books on the Vatican and Catholic affairs, and a popular speaker both in the United States and abroad.

The London *Tablet* has called Allen "the most authoritative writer on Vatican affairs in the English language", and renowned papal biographer George Weigel has called him "the best Anglophone Vatican reporter ever".

When Allen was called upon to put the first question to Pope Benedict XVI aboard the papal plane *en route* to the United States in April 2008, the Vatican spokesperson said to the Pope: "Holy Father, this man needs no introduction". That is not just a Vatican judgment. Veteran religion writer Kenneth Woodward of *Newsweek* described Allen as "the journalist other reporters, and not a few cardinals, look to for the inside story on how all the pope's men direct the world's largest church".

Allen's work is admired across ideological divides. The late liberal commentator Fr Andrew Greeley called his writing "indispensable", while the late Fr Richard John Neuhaus, a conservative, called Allen's reporting "possibly the best source of information on the Vatican published in the United States".

Allen's most recent book is *The Francis Miracle: Inside the Transformation of the Pope and the Church*. John divides his time between Rome and his home in Denver, Colorado. He grew up in Western Kansas, and holds a Master's degree in Religious Studies from the University of Kansas.

Jocelyn Bignold

Jocelyn Bignold is the CEO of McAuley Community Services for Women, an organisation which provides support, advocacy and accommodation for women and their children who are experiencing homelessness, primarily as a result of family violence or mental illness. Jocelyn has over 25 years' experience in community services, policy development, management and advocacy.

McAuley Community Services for Women is considered a lead organisation within the family violence and homelessness sector, and is widely recognised for its innovation, particularly in the areas of children and employment.

Frank Brennan SJ AO

Frank Brennan is a Jesuit priest, professor of law at Australian Catholic University and adjunct professor at the Australian Centre for Christianity and Culture, the Australian National University College of Law and the National Centre for Indigenous Studies. He is the National Director of Human Rights and Social Justice for Jesuit Social Services, and superior of the Jesuit community at Xavier House in Canberra.

His research interests encompass conscience and faith, human rights and the rule of law, and the rights of Indigenous peoples and asylum seekers. His recent books include *No Small Change*, *The Road to Recognition for Indigenous Australia*, *Amplifying That Still, Small Voice* and *The People's Quest for Leadership in Church and State*.

An Officer of the Order of Australia for services to Aboriginal Australians, particularly as an advocate in the areas of law, social justice and reconciliation, he was the recipient of the Migration Institute of Australia's 2013 Distinguished Service to Immigration Award and of the 2015 Eureka Democracy Award in recognition of his role in strengthening democratic traditions in Australia. The National Trust has classified him as a Living National Treasure. In 2009 he chaired the Australian National Human Rights Consultation Committee.

Helen Burt

Helen Burt is currently Policy Advisor with Catholic Social Services Victoria. She has worked for nearly 30 years in the community sector, mostly in faith-based organisations. In that time Helen's roles have included program development, policy work and management. Her work has focused on support and empowerment of the most marginalised and disadvantaged people in the community. In her career Helen has sought to develop service responses that are respectful of each person's needs, aspirations and essential dignity.

Al Curtain

Al Curtain is a Director on the Board of Mackillop Family Services. He was the Convenor of the Ethos and Culture Sub-Committee from 2011-2015 and is currently a member of the Research and Advocacy Committee.

Al is also currently the Senior Practitioner with SHINE, an Early Intervention Children's Mental Health team based in the City of Casey (Cranbourne) which is owned by a community controlled organisation called Family Life.

Al's qualifications include Bachelor of Theology (MCD 1997), Graduate Diploma in Adolescent Health and Welfare (Melbourne 2001) and Master of Law (Workplace Employment Law) (Monash 2006). For a period of five years he was involved in the Melbourne Young Christian Workers, initially in a full-time capacity and then as part of the leadership team. From 2001-2006 he worked for retail union the Shop Distributive and Allied Employees' Association. He was then with the Ardoch Youth Foundation as the National Corporate Relationships Manager until 2012.

Al is a care leaver from St Joseph's Babies Home in Broadmeadows and St Joseph's Children's Home in Surrey Hills. He has a lived experience of the out-of- home care system through experiences in residential care homes, family group homes and foster care placement. Al is a passionate advocate for social justice.

Julie Edwards

Julie Edwards joined Jesuit Social Services in 2001. She was the Program Director prior to her appointment as CEO in June 2004. Julie has over 35 years' experience engaging with marginalised people and families experiencing breakdown and trauma. She is a social worker, family therapist and a grief and loss counsellor. Julie holds a Master of Social Work and is currently completing her doctorate in this field. In January 2010 Julie became a Graduate of the Australian Institute of Company Directors.

Significantly, Julie has served on a number of government and philanthropic committees that work to promote a more just society and contribute to the health and wellbeing of members of our community. She is also a member of the International Working Group on Death, Dying and Bereavement and a member of a number of national and international Jesuit commissions and working groups across the areas of justice, education, social ministry, ecology and governance of natural and mineral resources. Julie is passionate about finding ways to give practical expression to her social justice values, exploring the most effective means to build a more just society and promoting a values-based model of leadership.

Bishop Mark Edwards OMI

Mark Edwards' family settled in Glen Waverley where he met the Missionary Oblates of Mary Immaculate while studying at Mazenod College, Mulgrave. After obtaining his Bachelor of Science from Monash University in Melbourne in 1980, he entered the Oblates and completed his ecclesiastical studies at Catholic Theological College, Melbourne, being ordained a priest in 1986. Later, Fr Edwards continued his studies at Monash University, obtaining a Doctorate in Philosophy. He worked as a teacher in Oblate secondary schools for 11 years. From 1998-2010 he held a number of positions in the Oblate formation community, St Mary's Seminary in Mulgrave. Fr Edwards also worked as a lecturer at Catholic Theological College from 2005-2010.

In 2010 Fr Edwards became Rector of Iona College from where, in late 2014, he was appointed Auxiliary Bishop of Melbourne being placed in the eastern region of the diocese. Bishop Edwards is also Episcopal Vicar for Tertiary Education and for Youth.

John Falzon OAM

Dr John Falzon has been the Chief Executive Officer of the St Vincent Paul Society National Council of Australia since 2006 and a poet since 1973. He is an advocate for social justice and has written and spoken widely in the public arena on the structural causes of inequality in Australia. He is the author of *The Language of the Unheard* (2012) and has worked in academia, in community development and in social analysis and research.

Denis Fitzgerald

Denis Fitzgerald is Executive Director of Catholic Social Services Victoria. In that role, over the past eight years, Denis has been involved in working with member organisations in public policy advocacy, strengthening cooperation within the sector, and reflecting with members on Catholic identity and its implications for Catholic social services.

Denis' academic qualifications are in philosophy, accounting and public policy. His career has included work in international relations, public policy and the delivery of government services, including three years as Australia's High Commissioner to Nauru. Denis also worked in taxation and consumer protection roles with the Victorian Government.

Social justice has been an enduring focus of Denis' career, including justice between countries, a fair taxation system, effective consumer protection and assisting the Church in Victoria to work for a more just and compassionate society.

Robert Fitzgerald AM

Robert Fitzgerald is currently a Commissioner on the Royal Commission into Institutional Responses to Child Sexual Abuse and is on leave from the Productivity Commission, where he has been serving as full-time Commissioner since January 2004. Prior to his appointment to the Productivity Commission, Robert was the Community and Disability Services Commissioner and Deputy Ombudsman in New South Wales.

Robert has a diverse background and extensive experience in commerce, law, public policy and community services including extensive involvement in numerous not-for-profit agencies. He is inaugural Chair of the ACNC Advisory Board.

Maria Harries AM

Maria Harries is Adjunct Professor at the Curtin University School of Occupational Therapy and Social Work and a Senior Honorary Research Fellow in the School of Population Health at The University of Western Australia. Her professional life has generally focussed on child and family welfare and mental health in both the government and non-government sectors nationally and internationally. She is currently a member of the Catholic Church's Truth Justice and Healing Council.

Alongside her own consultancy business, she continues her work as a researcher and research supervisor and holds governance roles with a number of state and national organisations involved with health, mental health, church, adult survivors, and child, adult and family welfare.

Ricki Jeffrey

Ricki Jeffery is currently the Diocesan Director of Centacare Central Queensland and working to develop strategies based on research and evidence to ensure CentacareCQ is sustainable and continues to provide services to the communities it serves. With a split focus on the present, near future and long term, Ricki is responsible for CentacareCQ's activities meeting current needs, preparing for medium-term demand and paving the way for long-term sustainability.

Previously, Ricki has worked in regional economic development gaining experience in regional Australian and American communities and investing in civic engagement, looking at capacity not deficiency, and coaching community leaders.

Donella Johnston

Donella Johnston is a passionate advocate for women in the Catholic Church in Australia. She currently holds the position of Director of the National Office for the Participation of Women at the Australian Catholic Bishops Conference. The Office's role is to promote the participation of women in decision-making, leadership and ministry and to ensure that the voices of women are heard by the Bishops of Australia.

She holds a degree in Arts/Asian Studies from the Australian National University, a Graduate Diploma in Secondary Education from the University of Canberra and a Master of Religious Education from Australian Catholic University. She has recently completed her Diploma in Management through YWCA Canberra. Donella has served on the Commission for Women for the Archdiocese of Canberra and Goulburn (2007-2009) and is a member of the ACT Government's Ministerial Advisory Council on Women. Her background is in Catholic education where she worked as a teacher, Religious Education Coordinator and Education Officer for the Catholic Education Office.

Donella is an enthusiastic life-long learner. She relaxes with Christian meditation, yoga, bush-walking, travel, gardening and spending time with her family and friends. She is an avid reader and enjoys art, music, theatre and cinema. Donella values diversity, inclusivity, authenticity and working in a vocation that supports and nurtures her spirituality.

Gerard Jones

Gerard Jones is the Director of Innovation and Business Development and Deputy CEO for MacKillop Family Services, a leading provider of specialist services to vulnerable and disadvantaged children, young people and their families in Victoria, New South Wales and Western Australia. During his five years at MacKillop, Gerard has held a number of roles including the National Director of Operations for three years.

Gerard has over 19 years' experience in the community sector, previously working for the Department of Human Services, Victoria where from 2006-2010 he managed the policy and program area for residential care and oversaw the development and implementation of the new therapeutic residential care model and championed access to education services for children and young people in out-of-home care. Gerard is a member of the Centre for Excellence in Child and Family Welfare Board.

Charlie King OAM

Charlie King is a sports commentator with the ABC. As a broadcaster, Charlie was the first Indigenous Australian to commentate at an Olympic Games, namely in Beijing 2008. His high sporting profile gives Charlie leverage to support the causes about which he is passionate. Active in promoting anti-domestic violence, in early 2006 he began talking with men about drivers of violence and engaging men in conversations about how they could take a more proactive role in starting to change men's attitudes about women and violence. Charlie is the Founder of the Territory-born, national campaign, NO MORE to family violence. The NO MORE campaign includes addressing prevention of violence through a whole-of-community approach and then drills down to working with individual sporting clubs to develop domestic violence action plans.

Charlie has been working in partnership with CatholicCare NT since 2006, developing strong men's programs and the NO MORE campaign. His work has been recognised through a range of national and Territory-level awards, including NAIDOC, Darwin City Council Citizen of the Year and Rotary awards, and in 2015 he was given an Order of Australia Medal for his services to broadcast media and the Indigenous community. Charlie became a board member of Our Watch in 2014.

Anne Kirwan

Anne Kirwan is the CEO of CatholicCare Canberra & Goulburn, and has been in community welfare for over 20 years. She is a registered psychologist who has worked within and managed various portfolios in services such as mental health, counselling, homelessness, youth, employment, comorbidity, disability and aged care. She is currently completing her Master of Business Administration.

Anne has been leading CatholicCare Canberra & Goulburn in its preparation for and transition into the National Disability Insurance Scheme. This significant shift in the provision of disability services has required strategic and operational leadership as the agency adjusts to a new operational environment. A key focus has been how CatholicCare maintains its mission, identity and values-based approach to care in this evolving marketplace.

Paul Linossier

Paul commenced as CEO of Wesley Mission in December 2015. He trained in Social Work at Monash University. Subsequent appointments included leadership of Harrison Youth Services, Kildonan Child and Family Services, Moreland Hall and Orana Family Services. For five years he had a consultancy practice, specialising in strategic planning and organisational review. In 1997 he was appointed founding CEO of MacKillop Family Services which he led until 2009.

Paul is a Life Member of the Centre for Excellence in Child and Family Welfare and past Chairperson of Catholic Social Services Victoria. He was awarded a Centenary Medal for services to the welfare sector and in September 2007 the Robin Clark Memorial Award for Inspirational Leadership. He completed the ANZSOG Executive Master of Public Administration in 2008.

Paul was an Executive Director and then Acting Deputy Secretary with the Department of Education and Early Childhood Development in the period 2009-2012. From June 2012 he co-led the whole-of-Government Vulnerable Children's Strategy team and in 2013 led the establishment of the Foundation to Prevent Violence against Women and their Children. In January 2014 he became inaugural CEO of the Foundation, which has been renamed Our Watch.

Jayne Lloyd

Jayne Lloyd has lived in the Northern Territory for over 30 years and worked in the social services sector for 20 years, the majority of this time as Director of CatholicCare NT. Jayne is a social worker by profession. CatholicCare is a significant social services agency in the Northern Territory with over 200 staff, delivering a broad range of services across regional and remote areas of the Territory.

Bishop Vincent Long OFMConv

Until his appointment in May 2016 as Bishop of Parramatta, Vincent Long van Nguyen was Auxiliary Bishop of Melbourne. In 1983 he became a Conventual Franciscan friar, studying for the priesthood in Melbourne. After his priestly ordination in 1989, he was sent to Rome for further studies and was awarded a licentiate in Christology and Spirituality from the Pontifical Faculty of St Bonaventure.

Bishop Vincent lived his childhood in poverty and war in Vietnam and spent many nights bundled into a bomb shelter under their home with his siblings and parents. He was 18 years old when he fled communism in 1980, travelling in a 17-metre boat with 147 other people. After eight terrifying days, he and all 147 other people made it safely to Malaysia.

Lisa McDonald

Lisa McDonald is the Director of Mission at St Vincent's Hospital, Melbourne. In this role, she has a broad range of responsibilities including leading and facilitation of mission formation and liturgies as well as ensuring staff and patients are inspired by, and understand, the Hospital's Catholic identity and values. Her role involves oversight of a number of programs including Pastoral Care and Chaplaincy, Aboriginal

Health, Volunteers, the Archives, the Art Program, Briar Terrace, social justice and cultural diversity initiatives, and events.

Lisa commenced employment in community media and worked as a TAFE teacher and Volunteer Manager in local government before pursuing opportunities in corporate training and then in ministry. She commenced her path towards Catholic health and mission leadership following her graduation in 1996 from a Communication (Journalism) degree. On completion of her master's degree in Theological Studies, Lisa and her family moved from Sydney to Melbourne for Lisa to take up her current appointment.

Her previous ministry roles in the Catholic Church have included Parish Youth Worker, Archdiocesan Youth Ministry Consultant for the Archdiocese of Sydney and Parish Pastoral Associate before joining the St Vincent's Health Australia family as the Mission Integration Manager at its Darlinghurst campus in Sydney. Lisa was appointed to the Board of the Caroline Chisholm Centre for Health Ethics in October 2011 and took up the role of Chair in February 2016.

Julian McMahon

Known as a human rights advocate and opponent of the death penalty, barrister Julian McMahon inspired conference attendees by addressing a range of social justice and human rights issues facing contemporary Australian society. He is a member of the Board of Jesuit Social Services and President of Reprieve Australia. Julian was admitted to the Victorian Bar in 1998. Articulate and measured, with longstanding community involvement, Julian has for more than 13 years worked without payment for Australians and others facing the death penalty. His clients have included Van Tuong Nguyen in Singapore, George Forbes in Sudan and members of the Bali Nine, Andrew Chan and Myuran Sukumaran.

Gabrielle McMullen AM

Professor Gabrielle McMullen is a Trustee of Mary Aikenhead Ministries, which was established at the instigation of the Sisters of Charity of Australia to continue their health and aged care, education and social service ministries. Since November 2015 she has also been one of three lay members of the Governing Council of the Missionary Sisters of Service.

Previous to this, and following postdoctoral research in Germany, Gabrielle joined Monash University and also became Dean of its Catholic residence, Mannix College, in 1981. She was then Rector of Australian Catholic University's (ACU) Ballarat campus from 1995-2000 and its Pro- and Deputy Vice-Chancellor (Academic) until February 2011.

Gabrielle has a long-standing interest in the identity and mission of Catholic agencies; she chaired ACU's Identity and Mission Committee for over a decade and convened the four cross-sectoral colloquia on identity and mission in Church-based organisations which were hosted by ACU in 2007-2010. She was awarded Member of the Order of Australia in 2012 and is a Fellow of the Royal Australian Chemical Institute and a Dame of the Order of Malta.

Marcelle Mogg

Marcelle Mogg has been CEO of Catholic Social Services Australia (CSSA) since July 2014. CSSA is the Catholic Church's peak body for social services in Australia, representing 59 member organisations which serve over one million Australians each year, in metropolitan, regional, rural and remote communities.

Marcelle is an energetic advocate for disadvantaged Australians and for the community and not-for-profit sector. In addition to her extensive experience in the development of policy, strategy and programs to support organisational growth and development, she has experience at board level of several not-for-profit services.

Marcelle's previous experience includes working as the acting Group Leader Mission and the Group Communications Manager for St Vincent's

Health Australia. She has also worked as the Director of Mission at St Vincent's Hospital, Melbourne and the Lay Partnership Coordinator for the Marist Brothers.

Marcelle has a Master of Business Administration (MBS), Bachelor of Social Science (Pastoral Studies) and Diploma of Applied Science (Nursing).

Tomasa Morales

Tomasa Morales is the Manager of Refugee Settlement Services at CatholicCare South-Eastern Melbourne, where her work focuses on supporting vulnerable individuals and families from recently arrived communities. Her work in this role has been recognised by awards from CatholicCare Melbourne and Catholic Social Services Australia; this includes winning the 2015 Fr Gerard Dowling Award in recognition of outstanding modelling of the mission and values of CatholicCare.

Prior to moving to Australia with her family, Tomasa was active in advocating for and supporting those impacted by conflict in El Salvador. Her contributions included, from 1986-1996, Presidency of CRIPDES, an organisation with a base of 300 rural communities in El Salvador, formed to assist refugees and displaced and other war victims from the countryside suffering human rights abuses. In 1990 Tomasa received the Prize of Solidarity from the Senate of Bremen in Germany, which was awarded to CRIPDES in recognition of its work in the defence of human rights.

Tony Nicholson

Tony Nicholson is Executive Director of the Brotherhood of St Laurence in Melbourne. He has dedicated over 30 years to improving conditions of those living on or close to the edges of society. A feature of his work has been his ability to collaborate with colleague social justice organisations, governments and businesses to achieve reform in public policy and service delivery for the benefit of disadvantaged Australians. Tony brings to the task of leadership at the Brotherhood a strong record of service development and innovation, research and policy analysis, and compelling advocacy on behalf of those disadvantaged in our community.

Michelle Reid SGS

Michelle Reid is a Catholic religious who belongs to the Congregation of the Sisters of the Good Samaritan. She has primarily worked in education in Australia but also trained in community development work and spent 10 years overseas. During these years she worked in the Philippines empowering women and families who lived in the slum areas and seeking their better education and livelihood as well as in formation of young Filipinos women interested in religious life. Michelle worked in Timor Leste from 1999-2006, mainly in the men's prison in Dili providing rehabilitation programs for the men as well as providing English classes for many Timorese. This was a life-changing experience and the beginning of many new journeys.

Michelle returned to Melbourne, her birthplace, in 2007 to manage the Good Samaritan Inn, a crisis accommodation house for homeless women and children, many of whom are escaping family violence. She enjoys the challenges and richness of living in such a multicultural city and working with disadvantaged women and children of all cultures.

Patrice Scales

Patrice Scales has held senior management positions in the private, public and-not-for-profit sectors for over 30 years, both as a communications specialist and in general management positions. For the past ten years she has worked in the not-for-profit sector as a consultant, writer and volunteer. She has a Bachelor of Arts and a Master of Arts (Communications), and is a Member of the Australian Institute of Company Directors.

Patrice was Chair of Council of Catholic Social Services Victoria from 2012-2016 and has been a Board member of a number of Catholic social service organisations including MacKillop Family Services, CatholicCare Victoria Tasmania, and Sacred Heart Mission. She was recently appointed to the National Council of Caritas Australia.

Ché Stockley

Ché Stockley is a legally trained policy specialist with over twenty years' experience working in the community, government and legal sectors. Ché has worked as MacKillop Family Services Senior Policy Officer for five years, specialising in evidence-based social policy analysis, in relation to children, young people and families.

Deb Tsorbaris

Deb Tsorbaris is CEO at the Centre for Excellence in Child and Family Welfare, the peak body for child and family services in Victoria. She has previously held senior roles in the Department of Human Services, Victoria and as CEO of the Council to Homeless Persons from 2003-2009. She holds a Master's degree in Policy and Human Service Management, Social Policy and Research from RMIT University.

Deb is deeply committed to fulfilling the aspirations of Victorian vulnerable families to have more opportunities for their children, through working to put children and families at the centre of Victorian government human services programs and policy work.

Michael Yore

Michael Yore is a consultant to both the education and social services sectors, providing professional development days in the areas of theology, mission and identity, Catholic Social Teaching and leadership development for Catholic organisations, schools and parishes. Michael has a background in theology and social work. For over 20 years he was Chief Executive Officer of Good Shepherd Youth and Family Service and later Director of Mission for the schools and welfare organisations auspiced by the Sisters of the Good Shepherd in Australia and New Zealand. He currently works with schools and parishes as well as providing ongoing consultancy services on behalf of Catholic Social Services Victoria and its member organisations. Michael is married with four adult children.

Acknowledgements

Many people and organisations contributed to the development of this book.

Firstly, we are indebted to the authors, most of whom presented their material at the Catholic Social Services conference entitled *Review, Reimagine, Renew: Mission making a difference in a changing world*, held on 24-26 February 2016 at the Catholic Leadership Centre in Melbourne; and who have subsequently revised their material for publication.

In addition to the authors of the various chapters, the following people assisted with the preparation of chapters for the book: Kylie Burgess, Fiona Power, Antony McMullen, Lucia Brick, Fiona Basile, Michael Yore and Peter Hudson. Their assistance is very much appreciated.

The welcome and positive contribution of Anthony Cappello and his colleagues at Connor Court Publishing includes that they made the development of the book very straightforward.

The conference out of which the book emerged was organised by Catholic Social Services Victoria, in partnership with Catholic Social Services Australia. We are grateful to the participants in the conference from across Australia, who contributed to the discussion of the ideas that were presented.

The Steering Committee for the conference was chaired by Denis Fitzgerald and included Michael Yore, Jenny Glare, Rev Jim Curtain, Tiffany Orbien, Gabrielle McMullen, Patrice Scales, Peter Hudson, Marcelle Mogg, Kylie Burgess, Janet Cribbes and Peter Richardson, with Committee members contributing to the event in many ways. In addition, Lucia Brick led staff and volunteers in conference administration, with significant contributions also by Antony McMullen, and staff of the Catholic Leadership Centre. Communications support for the conference was provide by very professional staff from the Australian Catholic Bishops Conference, *Eureka Street*, and the Catholic Archdiocese of Melbourne.

The conference, and thus the book, was made possible by support from the following sponsors, whose contributions are gratefully acknowledged:

- Archdiocesan Development Fund, Archdiocese of Brisbane
- Australian Catholic University
- CatholicCare Sandhurst
- Catholic Church Insurances
- Catholic Development Fund, Archdiocese of Melbourne
- Catholic Development Fund, Archdiocese of Sydney
- Catholic Education Melbourne
- Catholic Super
- Diocesan Development Fund, Catholic Diocese of Parramatta
- Jesuit Social Services
- Sisters of St Joseph of the Sacred Heart
- Villa Maria Catholic Homes

The editors, on behalf of Catholic Social Services Victoria, express their thanks to all these contributors, to whom the broader Catholic community of service is indebted.

www.ingramcontent.com/pod-product-compliance
Lightning Source LLC
Chambersburg PA
CBHW071841230426
43671CB00012B/2026